Essays on Citizenship

Bernard Crick

Continuum
London and New York

Continuum
Wellington House
125 Strand
London WC2R 0BB

370 Lexington Avenue
New York
NY 10017–6503

First published 2000

British Library Cataloguing-in-Publication Data
A catalogue record for this book is available from the British Library.

ISBN 0-8264-4821-6 (hardback)
    0-8264-4812-7 (paperback)

Typeset by Paston PrePress Ltd, Beccles, Suffolk
Printed and bound in Great Britain by Cromwell Press Ltd, Trowbridge, Wiltshire

.

Contents

'It is true that unity is to some extent necessary ... but total unity is not. There is a point at which a polis, by advancing in unity, will cease to be a polis: there is another point, short of that, at which it may still remain a polis, but will none the less come near to losing its essence, and will thus be a worse polis. It is as if you were to turn harmony into mere unison, or to reduce a theme to a single beat. The truth is that the polis ... is an aggregate of many members; and education is therefore *the* means of making it a community and giving it unity.'

Aristotle, *The Politics*

'I call therefore a complete and generous education that which fits a man to perform justly, skilfully and magnanimously all the offices both private and public of peace and war . . .'

'None can love freedom heartily, but good men; the rest love not freedom, but licence.'

Milton, *Of Education* and
The Tenure of Kings and Magistrates

'Teachers appointed to instil knowledge into the minds of citizens should not teach that which is false or noxious: the truth should be transferred in such a way so that those listening assent not from habit, but because they have been given substantial reasons, and hold human knowledge redundant, if it provides no gain for the life of man and citizen.'

Samuel von Pufendorf, *On the Duties of Citizens*, 1682

Preface

I begin with a candid and cheerful warning about what this book is not. It is neither a guide to nor a resource book for the practical delivery of the new subject 'Citizenship' in the National Curriculum. Such will follow, from the Qualifications and Curriculum Authority and other authors, as well as from a small cluster of non-governmental organizations ('The Citizenship Coalition') who have long been dedicated to promoting citizenship through and in schools and among young people generally. Neither is it a history. My new friend and associate David Kerr of the National Foundation for Educational Research (NFER) would be the best placed for this, perhaps building on the work of Derek Heater, the progenitor of the modern movement for citizenship in schools, who called me out of my academic cave in 1969 to see the light of a broader and neglected field.

Here are some essays old and new. Essays are not monographs: they aim to be speculative, thought-provoking and thoughtful, I hope; argumentative, sometimes polemical indeed and often informal in style, with a personal tone. Many people have influenced me but I speak for myself. Chapters 2 to 5 were all published in the 1970s and 1980s, setting out the general principles of what I call 'the false dawn' of the citizenship movement, most notably expressed in the report of a Hansard Society working party, published as *Political Education and Political Literacy* (Longman, 1978), edited by myself and Alex Porter with contributions from us both. Professor Ian Lister and I were joint leaders of the whole project which, in those far-off days before ever there was a

National Curriculum, began to spread as a voluntary movement, until following a change of government its forward march was halted – indeed in many schools forced into tactical retreat, at the least.

When I first looked back at those essays recently, which by the 1980s I had thought were, if not wasted effort, at best a very small piece of history, they seemed hardly relevant to the radically changed structure and system of public education. But then I saw that the *principles* underlying the concept of citizenship, its teaching and learning, had not changed, even if the modalities of their delivery have obviously changed. How could the principles change, indeed? As I will briefly show in Chapter 1, the ideas of citizenship are historically derived. My only caveat is that the connotation of 'political education and political literacy' was too narrow in the 1970s. 'Citizenship' conveys better than 'political education' the ancient tradition, long before the democratic era, of active, participative inhabitants of a state exercising both rights and duties for the common good, whether in official or voluntary public arenas.

The new essays are mainly personal reflections and advocacy arising from the report of the advisory committee set up by David Blunkett as Secretary of State for Education and Employment, *Education for Citizenship and the Teaching of Democracy in Schools* (QCA, 1998) – which I had the task of chairing; and about what followed, the statutory order for citizenship in secondary schools, and the guidance framework for 'PSHE and Citizenship' for primary schools. The last two essays may seem somewhat remote from questions of detailed practice in schools, but can show why *personally* I attach such great importance in our country to learning the practices of active citizenship from the earliest age as part of the good life in a better society. Citizenship, both the subject and the practice, should be a bridge between the vocational aims of education and education for its own sake, in danger of being forgotten. Not all of life is productive: there is leisure, there is culture, both of which active citizens can defend, indeed enhance. This book may, I hope, help teachers and all involved in education (governors, parents and even inspectors) gain or reinforce a sense of civic pride and mission, however much we all differ (and should) on the best way to deliver and use citizenship in different contexts. A sense of mission under-lies the new curriculum, for values and skills as well as knowledge, perhaps stressing values and skills more than mere knowledge (if knowledge is seen simply as information). David Blunkett has made this clear throughout. And this sense of mission must sometimes override as well as underlay any too literal or rigid reading of the details of the statutory curriculum, or even official guidance documents. After all, they both seek to stimulate critical and creative thinking.

The Citizenship Order 2000 applies, of course, only to schools in England, but the general principles of my arguments seem to me – again personally – equally relevant to the other constituent nations of our United Kingdom. Pupils in schools in England should realize that they are both British and English, but that the two identities, while compatible, are not identical; and they may have other strong senses of identity besides – perhaps regional, perhaps ethnic, perhaps religious, and certainly some sense of being a citizen of the world.

I have retouched some essays or addresses, rewritten and conflated others, but in the nature of essays and advocacy an unusual amount of repetition of key points has been inevit-able. The only justification for this is not Bellman's argument in Lewis Carroll's *The Hunting of the Snark*, 'What I tell you three times is true', but rather Jeremy Bentham's celebrated method, 'iteration, dissemination and reiteration'. Where I have felt the need to comment on and modify some of my arguments of the 1970s, I have added words in square brackets, rather than the easily missed ugliness of footnotes. When considering how far to retouch I have been irritated and a little ashamed to discover how casually back then I used 'he' to stand for 'she and he', but I have left nearly all these as they were not out of respect for what bibliographers call 'the integrity of the text', but rather to remind that some progress has been made.

Lastly, I do stress 'essays' and 'personally', for none of my views should in any way be attributed to the advisory group that I chaired, still less to what I have done or may have done (I find it hard tell) while advisor on citizenship to the DfEE. And this disclaimer, of course, applies to those whom I have relied upon and learnt from most in this field (I had a lot to learn): Derek Heater, Ian Lister and Alex Porter of yore, and more recently David Kerr, Jan Newton of the Citizenship Foundation, John Potter of CSV (Community Service Volunteers), Gabby Rowberry of CEWC (Council for Education in World Citizenship), Don Rowe of the Citizenship Foundation, Jenny Talbot of the Institute for Citizenship Studies and two public servants who cannot be named but who know who they are. Oh, and dozens of teachers and advisers whom I have met on the long consultation trail.

I am grateful to Thomson International Publishing Services for permission to reproduce essays of mine from Bernard Crick and Derek Heater (eds), *Essays on Political Education* (Falmer Press, 1977), and Pearson Education Ltd for later versions of some of those together with new matter in Bernard Crick and Alex Porter (eds), *Political Education and Political Literacy* (1978). A version of Chapter 7 has appeared in Nick Pearce and Joe Hallgarten (eds) (2000) *Tomorrow's Citizens: Critical Debates in Citizenship Education* (London: IPPR); Chapter 1 also appears in Roy Gardner (ed.) (2000) *Education for Citizenship* (London: Continuum).

Bernard Crick
Edinburgh
16 December 1999

1 A subject at last!

Dr Johnson once said, while considering in didactic session or lesson 'the nature of fancy', 'the purpose of life' and 'why were we born?', that the real question was 'why were we not born before?' Why, indeed, has it taken so long for England (not yet Scotland, Wales and Northern Ireland), unlike every other parliamentary democracy in the world, to make citizenship a statutory subject in a National Curriculum? To answer that would take too long, and others have stated the past and recent history of it (Heater, 1997; Kerr, 1996, 1999). I see it overall as a story largely of excessive national self-confidence: a sad reluctance, on the one hand, to accept that we need all kinds of adjustment to live decently and comfortable in our post-war and post-imperial skin; and, on the other hand, to get right down to educational earth, a belief that the *ethos* of the school was sufficient.

For the real trouble has been that the schools that shaped the mind-set of most governments and higher civil servants throughout the nineteenth century were the independent schools. They had a most effective ethos of education: for leadership – in the army, the imperial and home Civil Service, Parliament and the Church. Some still think they have, even if most of their products now head for 'the square mile' rather than the parade ground. The ethos stressed habitual loyalty and instinctive obedience to rules, call it at best respect for the 'rule of law', rather than critical thought and democratic practices. The idea of the good citizen could be found in this, certainly, but rarely the idea of the active citizen – that all subjects of the Crown should think of themselves as citizens

1

with rights to be exercised as well as agreed responsibilities. The English ideal of public service was, in other words, top-down. I like what Richard Hoggart has recently written, in sorrow more than anger, that not educating our young for the modern world through citizenship and critical thought is to hurl them 'into shark infested waters unprepared' (Hoggart, 1999). Not that that worries some of those who emerge from school with a deficit of human sociability quite happy to be sharks preying on others.

There was another version of the belief in the sufficiency of ethos: that if everything was participative, all rules made by or with the pupils, then formal teaching to prepare for active democratic citizenship is not merely redundant, but actually counter-productive. However, it is doubtful if this was ever put in to practice, except in a handful of eccentric independent schools; and even the prevalence of the ideology of progressivism in the 1960s and 1970s was much exaggerated. It was exaggerated grossly not merely by the stridency of its advocates but by the counterblasts of reactionaries and by sensationalism in the press blowing up bizarre happenings as general tendencies. As too often, moderates often kept too quiet – had a false tolerance for sincere nonsense (one of the mind-sets that I hope citizenship can change). Extremists feed off each other. George Orwell once said that the Peace Pledge Union (pacifist) was largely a consequence of the Navy League (somewhat bellicose). Peter Hennessey once called me 'a truculent moderate'. I have never thanked him until now.

We need both 'good citizens' and 'active citizens'. And teachers, if I may preach before being practical, need to have a sense of mission about the new subject, to grasp the fullness of its moral and social aims. The advisory group which produced the report, *Education for Citizenship and the Teaching of Democracy in Schools* (QCA, 1998) (hereafter called the 'Report, 1998') did not hesitate to state:

> We aim at no less than a change in the political culture of this country: for people to think of themselves as active citizens,

2

willing, able and equipped to have an influence in public life and with the critical capacities to weigh evidence before speaking and acting; to build on and radically extend to young people the best in existing traditions of volunteering and public service, and to make them individually confident in finding new forms among themselves.

But that is, indeed, an aim more than a definition. We in England have had considerable difficulties about the very concept of citizenship, let alone peculiar inhibitions. Our orators never say 'Fellow citizens . . .', and when nineteenth-century radicals did, it was meant to sound *almost* republican, somewhat French, somewhat American.

What is citizenship?

So let us try to be clear what we are talking about before considering the proposals for the curriculum. Important social and moral concepts always get defined in different ways by different groups for different purposes. They are what a philosopher has called 'essentially contested concepts'. That is why attempts to establish by social surveys what people think are moral virtues end up at least very ambiguous, almost meaningless if the observations cannot be correlated with behaviour (QCA, 1997). And definitions, whether by individual thinkers or by committees, do not settle arguments. 'Citizenship' can carry significantly different meanings. It has no 'essential' or universally true meaning, but one can attempt some reasonable understanding of the main usages of the term in our society and the great moral force behind what has come down to us historically. We can offer a working definition that will include the main contested usages. If no one can agree on any identical list of the virtues that might be thought either to constitute citizenship, or to be preconditions to it, yet the activity is not obscure.

Professor David Hargreaves has recently written:

3

Civic education is about the civic virtues and decent behaviour that adults wish to see in young people. But it is also more than this. Since Aristotle it has been accepted as an inherently political concept that raises questions about the sort of society we live in, how it has come to take its present form, the strengths and weaknesses of current political structures, and how improvements might be made ... Active citizens are as political as they are moral; moral sensibility derives in part from political understanding; political apathy spawns moral apathy.

(Hargreaves, 1997)

This puts it in the whole context of the history of political ideas, to which we are heirs and great beneficiaries. The activity or practice of citizenship can be universal (even if, alas, it still is not); but it had its origins specifically in ancient Greece and is a key part of our civilization. Historically there has been a fundamental difference between the concept of a citizen and the concept of a subject. Put simply, a subject obeys the laws and a citizen plays a part in making and changing them. To the Greeks and the Romans citizenship was both a legal term and a social status: citizens were those who had a legal right to have a say in the affairs of the city or state, either by speaking in public or by voting, usually both. But these citizens were always a proud minority: women were not citizens, there were slaves, and often a larger number of subject inhabitants who might have some personal and property rights in law or custom, but had no civic rights – that is, to vote and participate in public affairs. Active citizenship was believed to be a prime moral virtue: no human being could be themselves at their best without participating in public life. Aristotle remarked that whoever could live outside the *polis* – the city, or the civic relationship or the community of citizens – was either a beast or a god. Although both the Greek city states and the Roman Republic were destroyed, the memory and the ideal of free citizenship endured.

In the seventeenth century in England and the Netherlands this began to be called (following Italian jurists and writers of the Renaissance) 'civic republicanism', a term revived by modern scholars not to mean no monarchy (as Britain, The Netherlands, Sweden and others have constitutional monarchies) but because it describes societies where the public have, in the ideal of the Roman Republic, rights to be involved in the things that are of common concern (the *res publica*), and cannot merely exercise these rights but are presumed to have a civic duty to do so.

'Civic republicanism' is not a colloquial term. We now think of ourselves as a democracy. But the term can usefully remind us of several things. Firstly, that democracy as the idea of citizenship for all came late upon the scene, no earlier than the American and French Revolutions. Secondly, that in Britain it came even later and very gradually and peaceably through successive Reform Acts – despite some small if famous premonitions in the English Civil War. Thirdly, there was never any sudden break in our form of government, always carried on in the name of the Crown, to turn a consciousness of being subjects into a dramatic assertion that we were all citizens. So the term 'civic republicanism' could remind us that democracy is not simply the counting of opinions, but is reasoned public debate: the availability of information and a free press are as important as direct participation; neither can work well without the other. One of the reasons why education became compulsory was not just for the efficiency of the new industrial economy, but to make the expanding franchise workable. So seen in historical perspective, any education for citizenship must be compounded both of values and knowledge, as well as the skills that arise from early experience of discussion and debate.

Even in autocracies laws can be better or worse, and it can be argued that people should normally obey them, enjoy some rights and treat each other fairly: 'the good subject' under 'the rule of law'. But 'the good citizen' will be someone with civic rights in a democratic form of government, thus rights in law, who actually exercises them; and exercises them reasonably responsibly. *Good citizens will obey the law, but will seek to change it by legal means if they think it bad, or even if they think it could be better.*

Some of the difficulties we have had in England about the very concept of citizenship arose because until quite recently it was used almost always in a constitutional, legal sense: British citizens were seen as subjects of the Crown entitled to rights as established in law by ministers of the Crown. This concept is still of some importance: immigrants, for instance, seek citizenship in order to gain the full protection of the laws; and for the protection they receive, then they usually respect or at least obey the laws; and so within the laws a plurality of cultures and beliefs can coexist. But because in our history citizenship has more often appeared as something granted from on high to subjects rather than something gained from below as in the American, Dutch and French experiences, it has been very difficult for us to see the state as a contract between government and citizens rather than as a slowly evolving historical order. This downward-granting rather than upward-demanding perception of authority has had some unfortunate consequences for British society. Basic perceptions have tended to polarize, some saying firmly that lack of respect for authority is the biggest social problem, while others fasten on too much unquestioning deference. It was once believed that any specific education for citizenship was not needed – the whole ethos of authority in 'a good school' was enough; and if widely practised in the common or maintained schools might even disturb habitual respect for authority. But we will argue that education in citizenship can actually strengthen an authority that is exercised in a democratic context, resting on consent and an informed and reasoned mutual understanding. Authority, in other words, must seem relevant to felt needs. The pupil in school should go through a progression of necessarily being nearly wholly subject to becoming nearly full citizen. And having the vote at 18 is far from irrelevant in considering and restating the aims of education.

*Confusion has been endemic, however, between the idea of
'the good subject' and the idea of the 'good citizen'. They are
not the same.*

The report of 1990 of the Commission on Citizenship
appointed by the then Speaker of the House of Commons,
Encouraging Citizenship, did well to adopt and adapt as a
starting point the understanding of citizenship found in the
late T. H. Marshall's book *Citizenship* (Marshall, 1950). He
saw three elements: the civil, the political and the social:

> The civil element is composed of the rights necessary for
> individual freedom ... By the political element I mean the right to
> participate in the exercise of political power ... By the social
> element I mean the whole range from the right to a modicum of
> economic welfare and security to the right to share to the full in
> the social heritage and to live the life of a civilized being
> according to the standards prevailing in the society.

For the first element the Commission rightly stressed, more
than in Marshall, reciprocity between *rights and duties*. And
this led them similarly, regarding the third or social element,
to stress that welfare is not just provision by the state but is
also what people can do for each other working with each
other in voluntary groups and with local authorities in local
communities. Both of these they saw as a duty they called
'active citizenship'; but they had little to say about the second
element, the political element, and how that might be part of
education for young people whether in school or out of
school. Perhaps they took political citizenship for granted
(which it is not always safe for a society to do), but certainly
there was marked tendency at that time to take over the term
'active citizenship' to mean only, or mainly, civic spirit,
citizens' charters and voluntary activity in the community;
but not how individuals can be helped and prepared to shape
the terms of such engagements. Voluntary service, as well as
good in itself, is a necessary condition of civil society and
democracy, and should be a more explicit part of education;

but it is not a sufficient condition for full citizenship in our tradition.

So a workable definition must be wide, not because it aims to be all things to all men, but because it must identify and relate all three of Marshall's dimensions, not to call any one of them on its own true 'active citizenship'. Active citizenship should be interaction between all three. A submission from the Citizenship Foundation in response to the White Paper *Excellence in Education* (DfEE, 1997) made the same point:

> We believe that citizenship has a clear conceptual core which relates to the induction of young people into the legal, moral and political arena of public life. It introduces pupils to society and its constituent elements, and shows how they, as individuals, relate to the whole. Beside understanding, citizenship education should foster respect for law, justice, democracy and nurture common good at the same time as encouraging independence of thought. It should develop skills of reflection, enquiry and debate.

And always to remember that historically the practices of 'civic republicanism', free citizenship or free politics first arose in the world only when real differences of values and interests came to be accepted as natural or inevitable within a complex society. The business of politics and citizenship education alike then became not one of reaching some conclusive determination of values and of the ends of public policy, and then enforcing them; but to find morally acceptable compromises within agreed ways of conduct and acceptable procedures to resolve conflicts and difficulties.

Practical modalities

To come down to earth. What can we mean by 'effective education for citizenship'? Here I follow the 1998 Report – not surprisingly. To mean three things, all related, each mutually dependent on the others, but each needing a somewhat different place and treatment in the curriculum. *Firstly, children learning from the very beginning socially responsible behaviour both in and beyond the classroom, both towards those in authority and towards each other.* This happens in any good primary school – but not in all as yet, alas; so the base is there, or can be readily. *Secondly, learning about and becoming helpfully involved in the life and concerns of their school and their local communities, including through volunteering and 'service learning'* (we cannot say 'community service', the Home Office have criminalized that good term) *including voluntary service. Thirdly, pupils learning about how to make themselves effective in public life through knowledge, skills and specific values – what some have called 'political literacy'.*

David Blunkett in a speech of 7 July 1999 at the Institute of Education, London, made clear that the Order was to be, he said, 'light touch and flexible':

> We want to encourage schools to develop their own approaches, to be creative and to identify and use opportunities across the curriculum and beyond to enhance the teaching of citizenship. This will allow pupils to have the chance to exercise real responsibility and make an impact on school and communities. We are seeking nothing less than the encouragement of active and responsible members of tomorrow's community. Offering time for voluntary activities and bringing alive democracy at a time when cynicism and apathy is rife, is a key objective.

I gloss the reasons for 'light touch and flexible' (which stand deliberately in contrast to some of the other subject orders) as being both moral and intellectual but also political. Exercising 'real responsibility' is the best school of moral life and an essential condition for each individual's free actions to be compatible with, indeed enhanced by, those of others. And politically, in a free country, unlike in an autocracy, a citizenship education must not be centrally directed in detail, only in broad but clear principles. Government creates it, but puts it at arm's length. This is both wise and prudent.

9

Plainly the teaching of citizenship will make extra demands on some teachers – those who are not used to holding exploratory discussions on what the Report bluntly called controversial issues, but the Order more quietly calls 'contemporary events, problems and issues'. The direction that a free discussion can take is by definition hard to predict and at odds with a carefully prepared, sometimes too carefully prepared, lesson plan. And the order will make extra demands on some schools, those not used to interactive activities in the local community. Extra resources for both materials and in-service teaching are firmly promised. Some parts of the order, being knowledge based, will, of course, need formal teaching (one does need to know what one is talking about, and how to achieve worthy aims). And a definite allocation of dedicated time will be needed, whether weekly or in modules, even if large parts of the new curriculum *can* be delivered in conjunction with other subjects: history, geography, PSHE and RE, with English, maths and IT all making a contribution – as schools may choose and playing to their own strengths. I imagine that most head teachers will with their staff conduct an audit of what there is already, what can be adapted and what needs adding. If the Order is read carefully, the former can loom larger than many might think.

In primary schools citizenship is not statutory, but part of a skilfully revised new Framework of Guidance conjointly 'PSHE and Citizenship'. The Report identified three strands of citizenship which should occur in *each* Key Stage, but obviously 'social and moral responsibility' will loom larger to begin and 'community involvement' and 'political literacy' will expand progressively throughout the Key Stages. 'Responsibility' is an essential political as well as a moral virtue for it implies premeditation and calculation about what effect actions may have on others, care for what the consequences are likely to be and willingness to help repair the damage if the intended results go wrong – as can happen, as Robert Burns remarked, in 'the affairs of mice and men'.

Citizenship is important, it is a challenge; it raises difficulties, of course, where it has not been attempted before. The ambitions behind the Report and the Order make new demands on schools, but cannot possibly be delivered by schools alone. The advisory group said clearly that pupils' attitudes to active citizenship and their values are influenced by many factors other than schooling: 'by family, by immediate environment, the media and the example of those in public life. Sometimes these are positive factors, sometimes not.'

The example set by government and the media will not always be a great educator in civic virtues, but they must at least strive not flagrantly to contradict them. Example is a salient social mechanism. Kids notice. I was giving a talk on 'Parliamentary Democracy' once in a school sixth form class (to please an old student) when the head threw open the door and without a word of apology or courtesy, either to the teacher or myself, barked out a boy's name and had him out. That was better than a lesson on 'autocracy'. Kids notice if a head appears to consult with his or her colleagues, or just to tell 'em. I have not been privy to the reasons why the government moved so quickly on citizenship – probably for very much the same reasons stated in the advisory group's Report. Worries about alienation of many of the young from public values, low voting turnout in the 18–25 age group, exclusion and youth crime, and even where these unhappy conditions do not exist, a general, sensible feeling that it ill becomes a democracy any longer not to prepare its young to be both good and active citizens.

I doubt if the Prime Minister and the Home Secretary thought, 'Ah, it stands to reason that constitutional reform won't work in the long run without building a base from the schools for active citizenship, so let's give Blunkett his head.' But the logic of events points that way. The behaviour of the adult world, ambitions for both more *freedom* and more *responsibility* (how else can capitalism and democracy complement each other?) cannot be changed without preparation in the schools: a moral framework, relevant knowledge and practice in practical skills.

11

2 The introducing of politics in schools

The earliest version of this was the introductory essay in Derek Heater (ed.) *The Teaching of Politics* (Methuen Educational, 1969), which book marked the false dawn of the citizenship movement in the curriculum. I revised it for my first collection of essays, *Political Theory and Practice* (Allen Lane, 1971), and this text follows some further revisions in Crick and Heater, *Essays on Political Education* (Falmer Press, 1977). If the polemic against teaching 'The Constitution' is now dated, it may be because it had its effect gradually throughout all the examination boards. A new realism began to replace old Civics. But the reasons behind my polemic should still guard against any lapse back. Less pardonable was my ignoring of social studies at that time. The new citizenship is a creative synthesis of politics and social studies.

Since it cannot be avoided, it had better be faced. Since it should not be avoided, quite a lot of care and time should be given to it. And since it is an interesting subject, it should be taught in an interesting manner. Civilized life and organized society depend upon the existence of governments, and what governments should do and can do with their power and authority depends, in turn, on the political structure and beliefs of the subsidiary societies within the range of influence of these governments. To take a Greek or a Jacobin view of the matter may now appear to go too far: that a man is only properly a man when he can be a citizen and takes part in public life. But it remains true that a man is still regarded as less of a man than he can be if he or she has no public spirit, has no concern for and takes no part in all the jostlings of self-interest, group interests and ideals that constitute politics and society. Only a few would maintain that the good life consists in the avoidance of public concerns; but nearly all would recognize that our whole culture or style of life is less rich, that is less various and shapely, and is less strong, that is less adaptable to change and circumstances, if people of any age group believe that they should not or cannot influence authority [or could not care less].

This may sound very abstract, but the implications for education are embarrassingly concrete. Any worthwhile education must include some explanation and, if necessary, justification of the naturalness of politics: that men and women both do and should want different things that are only obtainable by means or by leave of the public power, and that they can both study and control, in varying degrees, the means by which they reconcile or manage conflicts of interests and ideals. The point of departure is all-important. When we ask for direction, there are occasions on which we should receive the rustic reply, 'I would not start from here if I were you.' In practical life, we have to start from where we are: perhaps, if we are unfortunate, as an inhabitant of a state that conceives politics as either subversive and divisive, or as the implementation of a single and authoritative set of truths which are to be extolled, but not questioned. But in education in a reasonably free society (and education in its fullest sense can only exist in reasonably free societies), we are reasonably free, despite practical limitations of various kinds, to start from where we choose. So we should start with politics itself. If we start from some other point, and I will discuss some of these conventional and innocent-sounding points of departure – such as 'the constitution' or 'good citizenship' or 'reform' – we may risk either heading off in the wrong direction entirely or creating a positive distaste for the most positive and natural part of the journey. Faced with the growing 'alienation of youth' or the 'conflict of the generations', public authorities are likely to insist that schools put more time and effort into civics. But this could prove a Greek gift to teachers of citizenship, and it could easily make matters worse if constitutional platitudes of the 'our glorious Parliament' kind are thrust on an already sceptical youth, rather than something realistic, racy, down-to-earth and participative which focuses on politics as a lively contest between differing ideals and interests – not as a conventional set of stuffed rules.

If, indeed, one were to explore school studies intended to be preparatory to university, I would have to admit to some scepticism as to their value. Even if all existing A level syllabuses in 'British Constitution' were reformed, I would still not be unhappy for universities to have to start from scratch in teaching all the social sciences – with the sole and not very comforting exception of geography. In my own experience as a persistent first-year teacher both at the London School of Economics and at Sheffield University, where one could properly point to entrance standards which were among the highest in the country, it was rarely any advantage for a student to have taken British Constitution at school, often the contrary. And this was not simply because they thought that they knew it already, but because (as I will argue later) their minds were often astonishingly full of irrelevant and picturesque detail about parliamentary procedure and constitutional institutions, so that they had none of that inquisitive turbulence about the manifold relationships of ideas to institutions and to circumstances that is surely of the essence of a political education. Better to have done history, English and either mathematics or a foreign language, in our education, in our present ludicrously overspecialized sixth forms, or, in some reformed system, these and almost any other reputable subject. An interest in politics might more naturally spring from an old friend, current affairs, which should, in any case, be a prominent part of secondary education throughout the school. The tendency of the universities to try to get schools to do their work for them is deplorable. The social sciences should not enter into a competitive race with other subjects for compulsory prerequisite subjects: for one thing, this perverts the purposes of secondary education, and for another, it is quite unnecessary – the social sciences are popular enough already in higher education despite the absence of prerequisite requirements and of offerings in the schools on like scale to the older, established school subjects.

As a professor of Political Studies, I am interested in political education at the secondary level of education because it should be there both in its own right and in the public interest, not as a feeder to the university Moloch. A or O level British Constitution or Government and Politics have their justification in allowing at least a few to specialize as the climax of a good general education, not as new and necessary preparation for university in a subject or area of concern which should already have been experienced at many points in the school timetable. At some stage all young people in all kinds of secondary schools and in vocational courses should gain some awareness of what politics is about. In some schools it may best occur in Liberal, General or Social Studies hours actually labelled 'Political Education', but in others it can best be explored where it may more naturally arise – always in history, always in social studies, often in English when certain books (like *Animal Farm* and *Lord of the Flies*) are studied, and often in geography with its growing concern with conservation, environmental controls and local planning procedures and controversies. It is more important that all teenagers should learn to read newspapers critically for their political content than that they should have heard of Aristotle or know – may heaven forgive us all – why the Speaker's Mace is not on the table on Fridays. So the best age for a conscious political education to begin is the age at which children begin to read the newspapers anyway – their political puberty. And it should continue into people's careers. That so much General Studies in further education is, in fact, concerned with political and social problems, demonstrates the neglect in so many schools.

I maintain that we must all start from such a point, and

argue on its merits the case for helping children to understand what political conflicts are all about and what purposes they serve, not take refuge in some politically denatured British Constitution or 'Good Citizenship' (by whatever name that genteel god goes). There are three objections at least against beginning with 'the Constitution', and these objections also apply to beginning with 'good citizenship': (a) there is no such thing which is not itself a matter of intense political dispute; (b) it is usually just a subterfuge to escape nasty politics and usually does the very thing it seeks to avoid: insinuates partisan biases, none the less real for being oblique; and (c) it makes an interesting and lively subject dull, safe and factual (easy to test, indeed – but what is being tested beyond brute memory?).

Let us take the constitution first. Taught in a purely legalistic manner, a study of politics is hardly worth having (although, it is fair to add, it is hardly likely to have much effect either). The analogy between the difficulties of teaching about political and sexual behaviour is irresistible. Both are natural activities in which it is as proper for the child to be curious as it is for the school to take up the burden of teaching what is socially acceptable and what are conventional moralities. Some teachers and some parents wish strongly to avoid both or either of these things, while others conceive it their duty to be dogmatic – whether directly or indirectly; so the usual compromise or line of least resistance is to teach these things in a purely structural, anatomical or constitutional way. But in both spheres the proper role of education must be to create an awareness of *why* it is that some people regard these matters as either taboo or dogma, and to offer some practical protection to children by instilling not a knowledge of what is right or wrong (which is beyond most of us to presume to teach), but a knowledge of what society and the subgroups in which they may move regard as right or wrong. I think we often overestimate the difficulties of leaving some questions quite open, quite deliberately unresolved, without either shattering personal faith and trust in the teacher or encouraging a sort of

17

educational hypocrisy. As a political theorist, I seem to spend half my teaching life attempting to create a sense of the plausibility and practical importance of ideas that I do not myself accept as true either morally or empirically.

When I used to be asked by first year undergraduates, 'But what are your opinions, Prof.' I took a proper and politic care, first, to make a little sermon that this is in no way to settle any question; secondly, to be a little ironical at why my personal opinions are interesting to the questioner, and to explain that my skill which gives me some authority consists mainly in exposing bad arguments and answers, but does not extend as far as being equally sure that I can give true ones; and, thirdly, to give nevertheless an honest and reasonably full answer – although its fullness will naturally depend on the occasion and the context. I both can and should speak more freely and fully on contentious matters to students in a common room, a corridor, a cafeteria or in a bar than from the podium – or else I am a very dull dog; but I am no teacher if I use my classroom authority to be a preacher ('a hedge-priest for some doubtful orthodoxy', as Michael Oakshott once put it). For a teacher must explain why so many honest men worship the Devil, whereas a preacher is bound only to blacken him even if with that condescending type of tolerance which is the sign of not taking another person's views or behaviour seriously. We should encourage the holding of opinions – strong and firm opinions – but in ways that are open to argument and exposed to refutations. To have some doubt about all things is not to believe in nothing; we are sceptics because ideas are important, otherwise we would be mere cynics.

To teach the constitution is like teaching elementary anatomy or biology instead of the nature of sexuality. They may be necessary first steps, or collateral studies, but by themselves they would either be an evasion, or quite simply something else. Much British Constitution teaching in schools seems to me to be of the same nature: either nervous of politics, or a curious dedication to a vocational training in local government law or, still more odd, in parliamentary procedure – as if there was a massive shortage of clerks of the House of Commons rather than of citizens. There is no constitution in the sense the syllabuses usually assume (it is a concept invented to be taught to others), or rather there is only one in a highly abstract sense that is very difficult to grasp. We learn games best, after all, by playing them – rarely by reading the rules. We read about the rules or attempt to formulate them clearly only when we begin to play very much more often, or want to play better or to play in different company. The British constitution is those rules, formal and informal, by which we can practise the kind of politics that we have wished to practise. The conventions of the constitution have no legal force and cannot be reduced to precise formulations without intense political dispute. And it is important to be able to explain why. Let me digress slightly to give a concrete example. Most textbooks stated that it is a convention of the constitution, arising from Baldwin's selection as Prime Minister, that the Prime Minister 'shall come from' the House of Commons. Then there came the metamorphosis of the Earl of Home into Sir Alec (so that for a few days the Prime Minister was in neither House). Thus, at first sight, the constitutional rule was either wrong or, more likely, misformulated. So new editions hastily said that the convention is that the Prime Minister 'should not be in' the Lords, not that he must come from the Commons. This would make sense as a legal rule, and can be learned – as we oddly say – by heart. But then look what happened. Not only was Sir Alec defeated, as happened to Baldwin twice, but, unlike Baldwin, he quickly lost the leadership of his party – though a man personally popular and of great selflessness and sincerity. Why did he resign as leader? Fairly obviously, because he could not control his powerful colleagues in the House of Commons. Why could he not? Partly temperamental factors, perhaps, but all these factors were subsumed in his lack of experience of attempting to do so before or of seeing it done at all recently as a House of Commons man. In other words, the original formulation may still be best, if seen not as a quasi-legal rule but as a maxim drawn from political experience: leaders coming from the sheltered atmosphere of the House of Lords are unlikely to have had the kind of experience that in modern conditions would fit them to be able to control their followers in the far more stormy House of Commons.

I simply give this as an example of political thinking, a concrete example of what even Sir Ivor Jennings meant by saying that conventions are obeyed because of the political difficulties which follow if they are not. Is this really too difficult or too contentious a point to get across to 14 or 15-year-olds? I would think the question an impertinence to ask of school teachers, if I had not found it hard to get across to 20-year-olds and even to 50-year-olds – so fixed in some minds is the disjunction between the constitution (good and teachable) and politics (bad and amorphous).

Here is not the place to examine the reasons for dislike of politics – whether by the unpolitical Conservative who may wish to rise above it, the apolitical Liberal who wishes to protect from it everything he or she believes in, or those anti-political or revolutionary Socialists who see politics as the mark of an imperfectly unified society. But such mistaken sentiments assume a peculiar importance in education. Small wonder that politicians and educationalists eye each other so warily, each feeling that the other should keep out of the other's business, and yet each wanting something from the other very much – resources, on the one hand, and respect on the other. Plainly, nearly all educational progress makes peoples able to contribute more to the aggregate of social wealth and skills, but it also makes them less easy to be led by the nose, less respectful of authority – whether in politics or in education – simply by invocation of its name. The danger in states like ours is now, indeed, not lack of ability on the part of the people to contribute, nor any great popular desire to hinder, obstruct or radically change, but simply indifference, incomprehension, alienation, the feeling of a huge gap between what we are told and what we see, and above all between what we are told we can do (the influence of public opinion and every little vote adding up, etc.) and what we can in fact do.

Teachers of politics must themselves develop and thus be able to convey to others an intense sense that, as the good children would say, there are faults on both sides. This is as good a pedagogic fiction or framework as any and, since this is the basic problem of the relation between politics and education, it might be thought unreasonable to deny that it happens to be true. We need to be able to say at the same time, 'Look how they govern' and 'But look at how we educate about the business of good government'. A growing disillusionment with the government tends to increase either resistance to teaching politics at all, or, where it is taught, the determination to keep it narrow, safe and dull. But disillusionment with governments – and I take for granted that I am writing at a time [and still am] when no sane person can find more than a qualified enthusiasm for a party's performance or prospects – is a general phenomenon with three obvious aspects, none of which is to be ignored. People are disillusioned with actual governments and hence with politics because of (i) how government too often conducts itself; (ii) the inherent limits in which modern governments operate when sovereignty does not mean power; and (iii) people expecting too much. These factors are all far more important than being sure that pupils 'know the constitution'. Someone has to explain them and gain sympathetic understanding. The Press does a good job, sometimes a rather destructive job, on the record of governments, but rarely creates any awareness and understanding of the second or third factors. For general factors like inherent limitations are never topical on the crazy day-to-day myopic basis which the Press regards as essential *to make* news; and the frustration of unreal popular expectations is too abstract a point when the great god News also has to be 'hard' and 'personal' as well as instantaneously topical. Perhaps it is the behaviour of politicians and political journalists which makes the teaching of politics, one should candidly admit, as difficult as it is important. They should be the first to explain the

21

limitations of resources, existing commitments and environment under which any government must suffer. And politicians should be the first to warn against hoping for too much. But they are usually the last to do this. Too often politicians talk down and seldom assume that ordinary people are capable of understanding the basic facts about the economy – if they are simplified intelligently. At that point the professions of politics and education should meet, but rarely do. The politician is at fault for neglecting to adapt to modern educational standards – as even Bagehot had called it – the 'educative function' of Parliament. The disputes between the parties are commonly conducted by intelligent men in a deliberately stupid and stupefying manner; and the public, including adolescents, seems well aware of this, often seeing politicians as figures of fun, especially at election time. But teachers are at fault for not trying to raise the level from below: they commonly teach 'the Constitution', but one can search the standard school books on the British constitution in vain for the simplest list of what have been the major policy disputes between the parties in recent years, or the simplest diagrams of national income and expenditure under different headings (which possibly suffer from the double handicap of being 'Economics').

If politicians will not be more candid, it is hard to blame teachers for being evasive, especially when they are thus starved of interesting, topical and realistic teaching materials. To this point we must return, but it suffices for the moment to suggest that sometimes dull and abstract books have to be used, which avoid the subject matter of political disputes and expound and extol highly dubious constitutional and legal limitations on government, simply in default of others more realistic. There is a dearth of simple, informative books of what one could call, by other names, Contemporary History or Current Affairs (and here, of course, most university level textbooks are completely unhelpful, even for the teacher, with its methodological rather than substantive or practical preoccupations).

22

The nature of politics demands that we should always teach and show the two sides of things: what we want the state to do for us, and what we wish it to be prevented from doing to us; or, quite simply, aspirations and limitations. For the one without the other is as misleading as it is useless. So it is not 'finding excuses' to talk more seriously than politicians commonly do of the nature of limitations. Indeed, to do so may protect children from that one great cause of radical disillusionment or alienation from politics that is simply a product of starting with quite unrealistic expectations. This can take a socialist form, of course, but can equally well take a liberal form, or what would be called in America a 'League of Women Voters', or here (once upon a time, at least) a 'Hansard Society' mentality [or what Australians call, 'nice Nellyism']. Even or particularly the idealist must remember that Pilgrim had to walk through both Vanity Fair and the Slough of Despond before he could attain the slopes of Mount Zion.

To give one more example. Rarely do the actual policies of parties figure much in teaching or classroom discussion – although any good journalist could give a reasonably objective and clear account of them. If policy is tackled at all, then a kind of halfway house of realism is gratefully found by reading and considering the party programmes. But to take programmes at their face value is positively to create disillusion. For we then measure the success or sincerity of governments in terms of whether or not they have carried out their programme – a kind of political football pools; and some actually denounce any trimming of the sails to changed winds as going against prior instructions or 'the mandate' (whatever that may mean) and, therefore, as arbitrary and undemocratic. Certain things have to be said first about programmes and manifestos in general before there can be any meaningful discussions of their relationship with the actual policies pursued by a government. They were, for instance, originally almost exclusively a part of radical and reformist politics in the twentieth century; they were unknown in the nineteenth

23

century except as socialist pipe-dreams; and the famous Tamworth Manifesto of Sir Robert Peel was simply an unusually elaborate 'election cry': it entirely lacked the comprehensive character of a programme, and, in any case, one lark does not make even a false dawn. The Liberals did not offer a programme until Lloyd George's unofficial Yellow Books of 1932, and Conservatives resisted having a comprehensive programme until as late as 1950 because, quite sensibly, they held that it was impossible to foretell the future and unwise to commit oneself to do things when circumstances might change. This followed from their [pre-Thatcherite] general view of politics as concerned basically with the management of existing interests based on long experience, rather than with deliberately fermented change. Programmes are essentially a reformist and democratic device; but then even democracy has its limitations: it is no verbal quibble but a profound truth that government itself cannot be democratic, it can only be restrained or even strengthened by democratic devices. Another point to be made is that, in any case, programmes commit parties but not governments. So the unmoralistic lesson is surely to show that if programmes are seen as promises, then it is odd, by analogy, to employ a man for a job solely on what he promises to do without also considering his record. If he appears to promise too much, while one will not necessarily hold it against him, one may sagely take his words with a pinch of salt, but only if his record is good. General elections, in other words, are not likely to be decided and nor should they be decided on programmes and promises alone, nor – in rapidly changing societies – on record alone; the record must show that someone is capable of adaptation and change. Again I put these points forward simply as an example of political thinking, and as realistic points that can be got across objectively and which are far more important, both from the point of view of civic morality and of conveying correct information, than knowing weird details of election law.

Again, is it too difficult to show that parties hold different views not just about what should be done, but about the facts of the case? In the above case, the radical believes that a general election decides a programme to be carried out, but the Conservative believes that a general election decides which group of men shall be trusted with the complex and shifting business of government. I do not think it a weak or evasive conclusion to state that it would be an odd and bad world in which either conclusion was pushed to extremes. For strong and definite words should then be spoken of the folly of applying the right theory in the wrong circumstances. But the teacher does not come down on the side of either or any theory or doctrine, but rather tries to show their inwardness, their plausibility. There is no prejudice in trying to show, to fish for a carefully matched pair of examples, that it was as politically unrealistic for the Conservatives to offer no real programme in 1945 as it was for Mr Wilson to saddle himself with over-elaborate programmes in the economic circumstances of 1964, 1966 and 1974.

What I argue for is the need for a more realistic study of whatever we call it, and I have no objection to a grand old name like 'The British Constitution' (God bless it and preserve it from all enemies!), so long as we tacitly translate this eighteenth-century, Whiggish phrase as 'The British Political System' or simply 'British Politics' (although the question does arise, to which I will return, why just British?). A political education should be realistic and should chasten the idealist. Ideals are too important to be embalmed; they must be wrestled with and confronted [confronted with other people's differing ideals], but fairly and openly. There is no room for evasion: as teachers we must openly argue with that kind of liberal who thinks that children should be protected from knowledge of politics, just as the grand old constitution tries to protect us from party politics; and should argue too with that sort of businessman who thinks that we could do without it, that 'political factors' spoil rational economic calculations, forgetting as he does that probably nine-tenths of the big decisions in industry are political in the sense that they arise

25

from distributions of personal power and influence rather than the logic of cost-accountancy.

A political education, too, should inform the ignorant; but realistically. Politics is, after all, like sexual activity, undeniably fascinating (and like sex education, it cannot just be a matter of anatomy). If we act as if it is not fascinating and controversial and offer instead largely irrelevant background or constitutional facts, then children either see through us or are suitably bored. But realism involves talking coolly about politics, not striking hot political attitudes. The teacher who goes on and on about the Mace, the stages of Public Bills and the difference between the powers of the House of Lords and of the House of Commons in the scrutiny of Statutory Instruments, is only slightly less of a menace than the few teachers (but their fame goes a long way) who treat British Constitution as a chance to [try to] indoctrinate students in their view of THE TRUTH. If sinners are far fewer than local education authority committees and school managers [and the Press] sometimes imagine, the varieties of sin are probably greater. I meet quite as many first-year students who cite schoolteachers for the authority that 'Mr Wilson has violated the Constitution' (to which I reply, 'first catch her'), as for the more famous view that '*The whole system* is grinding down the workers.' ('Especially', I allow myself the comment, 'the third of the working class who regularly vote Tory.')

It is all too easy to exaggerate the difficulties of a reasonably objective teaching of politics so that most institutional nervousness that studying politics means partisan debate is quite unnecessary. I say 'reasonably objective', however, because part of political morality, or the morality that tolerates real conflicts of opinion rather than seeks to stamp them out, consists in appreciating how much all our views of what we see in society are affected by what we want to see. This is no dark secret and nor should it make teachers worry that politics is not as objective – may one sometimes say, not as cut and dried – as some other school subjects: the element of subjectivity in perception is the basis of literature and art as well as of politics. We do not insist that one way of doing things is true. On the contrary, rational argument in politics and therefore in the teaching of politics follows a method of trying to show that on such and such an issue different people, who ordinarily see things rather differently, are for once, in fact, agreed. The artful Communist quotes *The Times* to support him and the shrewd Conservative the *Morning Star*.

The teacher's task is, at whatever level, primarily a conceptual one, not a matter of conveying an agreed corpus of factual information. He needs to build up and extend an elementary vocabulary of concepts through which we both perceive the world and use them to try to influence it. The teacher has, above all, to show the difference between talking about an opinion and holding it. And from this he or she can go on to show how and why political events are interpreted in different ways by equally adult people. Here, to speak without undue irony, British popular newspapers furnish excellent and readily available teaching materials. The teacher must then be able to convey imaginatively an understanding of the plausibility (or, as Harold Laski used to say, the inwardness) of different political doctrines, even using unusual and unpopular ones as examples. The teacher must illuminate differences, not seek to show that we are all really agreed about fundamentals – for we are plainly not, unless we have lost the capacity or inclination for thought. He or she is then in a position at least to avoid – even in the teeth of most of the textbooks – the most crippling and common of all errors in considering politics, the belief that institutions and ideas can be considered apart from each other, sometimes expressed as the difference between theory and practice. The teacher should show all institutions serve certain purposes and must be judged by how they fulfil them; and equally show that ideas, which do not seek some institutional realization, are not political ideas at all. It should be a part of the beginning of political education, not the end which few then reach, to accustom people to probe and to discover what are, in fact, the general ideas of people who claim to hold no abstract ideas and to be acting in a purely practical manner. Those who claim to have no time for theory commonly hold the most interesting, sometimes arbitrary, often quite fantastic, general views on how things work and should work. Think of all those who wondered what would happen to 'sovereignty' if we went into Europe, just as Rousseau, Lord North and Dicey once all thought that federal solutions were impossible. 'What do they really believe in?' and 'what do they really think they are doing?' are two questions that ordinary people, 'the People', should be taught to carry into every aspect of their dealings with authorities.

The teacher himself should not advocate one doctrine or another, even our 'British Way and Purpose' that was the title of a famous Army Education Corps manual during the Second World War. The teacher simply points out the kind of conditions which appear to go with certain ideas and the kind of consequences that appear to go with holding them. For children must surely be brought to see society, in however elementary a form, as a system or a pattern of relationships, so that the Conservative will typically say, 'Don't meddle – the unexpected repercussions will overwhelm you'; the revolutionary socialist will say, 'All or nothing, partial reform is impossible'; and many others pursuing limited objectives will try to reassure themselves that the unintended repercussions of their particular policies are either trivial or, with proper forethought, avoidable. Naturally the teacher must begin by teaching what the received political ideas of our own society are, and how they relate to the social institutions. But he must avoid implying any finality and superiority to our traditional but severely local arrangements; and it is hard to see how such implication can be avoided if, even or particularly at the beginning, some other system or systems are not also looked at, however superficially. I am not convinced that school-children need to know anything about the intricacies of parliamentary procedure; I am convinced that they should know something, however superficially, about how Russia, the United States, China and some countries of the Third World and of Europe are governed. The point is not to establish any hierarchy of institutions, either in our favour or to chasten insular pride; but simply to show that there are different sorts of relationships and that in none of them can political ideas of institutions be considered apart from their social or national setting; and it is precisely this that 'the Constitution over all' approach denies – to make this point for the last time.

Perhaps, however, a qualification or explanation is needed before proceeding. I would not suggest that some study of abstract models (for such they necessarily are) of institutional structure and of formalized customary rules does not have a place. But its place must follow and not precede some knowledge of the issues and traditions of actual politics. If it is put first, either in emphasis or in order of teaching, it is likely to distort understanding of government and politics to a degree almost, I find, beyond repair. For, after all and again, customary rules arise from political activity and experience, not the other way round; and the machinery of government is made and remade by men to serve their purposes; it is not a natural impediment.

A useful analogy is with modern methods of language teaching. Grammar is discarded as the way in, but it is then introduced at a later stage as a framework with which to consolidate and extend our existing knowledge. Few would now believe that the direct method alone suffices; some structure, whether called grammar (the constitution) or structural linguistics (categories of political behaviour), must follow. But at the moment there is little doubt that most horses find the cart firmly harnessed up in front of them, and one can hardly go too far in possible exaggeration to redress a balance already weighed down ponderously in precisely the wrong direction. Another common disguise or perversion of a study of politics is 'good citizenship': the use of civics or liberal studies classes to urge participation in this and that. Sometimes this may degenerate into crude moralism, and a

29

rather romantic and prissy one at that – of 'the people versus the politicians' or 'I wouldn't let my daughter marry a politician' kind. There is a type of civics which is straight early-nineteenth-century Liberalism, teaching or preaching that the individual should directly influence this and that and make up his own mind in proud and independent isolation (whether he is a humble citizen or elected representative); and that he should avoid like the plague parties, pressure groups, unions and all other 'organized interests' (as if disorganized ones were better). This is simply unrealistic, individualistic in a thoroughly antisocial and unsociological sense, and often highly partisan. One must gently insist that Liberals, whether of ancient or modern ilk, can be no more immune than Tories or Socialists from some scepticism that their own account of what politics is all about is, taken by itself, fully adequate.

The less obvious danger of the 'be good boys and girls and participate' kind of teaching is the more insidious: the assumption that participation is both a good thing in itself and the best possible thing. Since personal participation in national politics other than by simply casting a vote is plainly impossible for most people in societies as large as we need to ensure the benefits we demand, it follows that the teaching of participation as an end in itself is only likely to create disillusionment in practice – if it does succeed in influencing local activities [and all kinds of voluntary groups] and does not simply sound so much cold pie in the classroom.

The virtues of participation are an important half-truth, but a lame half-truth if advanced alone. The other and complementary half is quite as important: that people must know, however vaguely, what decisions governments make, how they are made and what is happening. Informed and wide-ranging communications are as important for democratic politics as is direct participation – which, in practice, only involves a few, usually the few who preach it. Governing authorities of all kinds are more apt to urge participation, because they know that in a widespread manner it is impractical, than they are to study how to make themselves govern more openly and less secretively. Governments are fundamentally restrained and directed in societies such as ours not by participant-represen-tatives (who are mainly the recruiting ground for members of the government), but by their knowledge that nearly every-thing they do may become a matter of public knowledge. Governments can ordinarily depend on their parliamentary support but only to a far smaller degree on their electoral support. And by the same token, the people's representatives can pass economic legislation and orders until they are red or blue in the face, but putting them into practice almost wholly depends on governments or other authorities being able to explain them and to obtain some response from the working population.

Knowledge of what is happening and how things happen is quite as important as theoretical opportunities for participa-tion. Therefore, both in the light of the subject itself and for its practical consequences, I have some scepticism towards the American-style teaching of democracy by way of fabricating democratic situations in the classroom through games, debates, mock parliaments and class elections, etc. These may be fun, may teach some political manners [and tolerance], may develop some expressive and advocacy skills and provide some stimulating alleviation of routine, but they can only supplement, not replace a realistic knowledge of how the real system works. Governments are as much restrained by know-ing that their acts are publicized as by participant devices themselves. The absence of political censorship and the presence of an independent Press are quite as important as free elections, and this should be said. When Aristotle talked about political justice he invoked two basic criteria: that we should rule or be ruled in turn – participation; and that the state should be no larger than that the voice of Stentor or herald could be heard from one boundary to another. Modern political ideas and theory have almost exclusively stressed the first criterion – as if abandoning the second as unrealistic, paradoxically at the very moment of time when mass commu-nications have rendered it readily applicable to huge states,

31

not just to small communities. Participation of persons and communication of knowledge must, in other words, go together.

Content must not be sacrificed for process. Even to play 'United Nations' is surely difficult if all the little countries or role-players have not some prior knowledge, however simple, of how their characters behave, both in New York and back home. Peanuts had it all: 'Charlie Brown, Charlie Brown, gee, you were dumb in school today.' 'I thought I did OK.' 'Nope, you were dumb, real dumb. You got everything wrong.' 'Guess I misunderstood. Thought one only had to be sincere.'

Ultimately that is the difficulty of all attempts to enliven the teaching of politics by remorselessly discussing nothing but 'how should things be reformed?' The question is meaningless, except to an anarchist revolutionary (not even to a genuine Marxist), unless it arises from a realistic knowledge of how things are actually done. The politically desirable can only be the sociologically possible (though not for one moment to deny that we differ politically in our judgements about what is possible politically almost as much as in our judgements about what should be done).

Plainly we in Great Britain can no longer take for granted, if ever we could, that people either here or elsewhere know or care much about our political institutions and ideas. The knowledge of ordinary people and school pupils about policies and ideas is abysmal. We were once famed for our political abilities and knowledge. We now worry that our own younger generation is becoming actively alienated or sullenly indifferent to our political institutions; and internationally we have grown noticeably more silent about being an Athens of example now that we are no longer a Rome of power. It is almost as if we now have to begin all over again, like the seventeenth-century Commonwealth men and the eighteenth and nineteenth-century radicals, rediscovering our alternative traditions and rethinking our possibilities. This can hardly begin too early, and it will surely fail or prove irrelevant if it is not done in a manner both stimulating and realistic. And this depends a great deal on the schools. To give children the lowdown on how political institutions work and what political conflicts are about, rather than the dry bones of parliamentary procedure or the elevated abstractions of 'the Constitution', will not be to feed disillusion or to encourage cynicism, quite the contrary: it will encourage ordinary young citizens (and I speak technically, not rhetorically, as the voting age moves closer to the classroom), their teachers and their politicians to think in terms of common problems to be solved, and to talk about them in common language, not to build up protective walls of mutual incomprehension. It will encourage them to think morally, what should be done; but to think realistically as well as morally: what should be done that is possible, what should be done in the context of other people's opinions of contradictions, difficulties and traditions.

Says the teenager, 'We are being got at again'; says the head teacher or chairman of the governors or of the examining body, 'This is dangerous ground, be very careful, stick to clear facts, cleave to the Constitution ... politics is not a real subject in educational tradition' (at which the ghosts of Aristotle and our great English Hobbes and Locke, and Anglo-Irish Burke and Mill should arise to haunt them horribly in rebuke for their ignorance); and says the politician, 'People do not understand what we are trying to do for them in very difficult circumstances, and blame us for mirroring their own divisions, doubts and uncertainties.'

The task of re-establishing a popular tradition of political discourse both critical and aspirant must begin in the schools and with teachers. And it will plainly have to precede a suitable literature. It is not my task or competence to review the literature on politics for schools – if it can be called such, for it is mostly about the structure of government and rules and conventions of the constitution, the dull and heavy statues of Prometheus waiting for divine touch of humanity. Nearly all such books that I know to be commonly used lack the two essentials of a political education: realistic accounts of how governments and parties work and critical discussions of political ideas, or of what should be done and how – the moral assumptions and preconceptions that people carry, necessarily but usually unrecognized, into practical activities. For instance, if teachers follow arguments of the seminal report *Colour and Citizenship* (Rose *et al.*, 1969) and lay stress on a tolerant perception of social differences rather than an assimilationist stress on common moral factors, they may soon find that there are better and more down-to-earth books being produced about the minority groups than about the English majority. But supply, being partly at least and often pleasantly venal, will inevitably follow demand – if the demand comes first, as indeed there are many signs, like the volume in which this essay first appeared (although this is certainly not for the children), that it is beginning to do. [As happily it now has – both supply and demand.] We all should love our subjects, or else, like benevolent autocrats, we are misplaced or are due to be replaced. But the teacher of politics can have some justification and pride in claiming that the subject has a peculiar combination of difficulty, importance and fascination.

3 On bias

This essay arose from an address given as President of the Politics Association to their annual conference in 1971 and from discussions afterwards. It was printed in *Teaching Politics* (May 1972), but this present version was amended for Crick and Heater (1977) and with a postscript added to review two important books on indoctrination published about the same time.

Many councillors, officials and parents would believe in principle that politics education should be in the school curriculum because it is so important to us all, but in practice oppose or obstruct because they also believe that it cannot be taught without bias. This poses an important and interesting problem that is both practical and philosophical. The answer is not easy. For to reply that it must only be taught factually and objectively is then to denature the subject into the kind of irrelevant dullness against which I have already complained; and even then is to give no lasting guarantee that a teacher will not pronounce 'the facts' with a sneer or with ecstatic benevolence. And scepticism about whether total objectivity is possible in politics might spread into what should be (but oddly seldom is) equally suspect, history. Were I a parent living in Ireland (North or South) I might well be, for instance, in favour of disallowing any history teaching in schools; and if I were living in Hungary, Poland or Czechoslovakia [in Soviet times], for instance, I might not, out of personal pride or principle, believe a word that I was taught – though I could do

Essays on citizenship

well in the examination, giving 'em back what they want, as
may Mrs Jones's Willie even.

The problem may, rather, be to distinguish between inevitable human bias, when others can see where we stand, but
can see that we are giving a truthful and recognizable account
of something; and gross bias, where others may either be
puzzled where we really stand or suspect that we are lying or,
at least, grossly distorting. To distinguish between mundane
and gross political bias, we have to go back to what we mean
by politics at all.

Politics is the creative conciliation of differing interests,
whether interests are seen as primarily material or moral. In
practice they are usually a blend of both. In all societies
known to history some differences of interests exist even in
the simplest tribal societies with minimal government and
even in the most complex and oppressive totalitarian regimes.
But only if it is accepted that it is natural for men to differ
about interests and ideals does politics cease to be something
furtive and residual, usually scorned and persecuted in autocracies however much practised, and become – in rare and
favoured historical circumstances – something public, tolerated, perhaps even honoured. Sometimes politics is even the
organizing principle of a society, as when there are actual
political institutions, representative assemblies and parliaments, which represent the attempt to maintain order and
justice (the primary business of government) amid diversity
(the primary condition of liberty) and also amid an increasing
well-being for every inhabitant (a specifically modern condition of stability).

It is necessary to begin so abstractly, to try to see what is
basic or prior to our particular form of parliamentary institutions, precisely in order to make a very concrete point. If
politics is the recognition and tolerance of diversity, so must
be a political or civic education. No wonder the young, in a
growing complicated society, sometimes rebel against, but are
more often cynical about, teaching which simply asserts the
values of our society, the consensus, the parliamentary system

36

and the constitution. In fact, we live in a society which represents a considerable diversity of values. Consider only the major religions and branches of Christianity: true that they have much in common, but we cannot take their adherents seriously if we ignore their great differences. There is always a case for toleration, for understanding something of which one disapproves so that one knows how not to overreact to it, how to practise forbearance, how to persuade but not to proscribe or persecute: but there is seldom a real case for an ecumenicity which obliterates all distinctions of doctrine. And the argument is similar for secular and political moralities, for they too are not one but many. To stress deliberately 'what we have in common' and to underplay differences is both a false account of politics and a cripplingly dull basis for a political education.

The consensus can be imposed and, if it is imposed, it is, indeed, oppressive; but if it is imposed, it is imposed for the sake of particular political doctrines, not for the sake of the maintenance of order as such: only in a minimal sense of adherence to rules of procedure is consensus a necessary condition of order. In the maximal sense of distinct moral systems, there have been many political systems, both free and unfree, which have survived for long periods of time amid the most vivid diversity of moral codes (our own, for example, but even the Roman, the Hapsburg and the Ottoman Empires). There are outer limits, of course, and what these are is a difficult, interesting but different question. It is simply not true, however, that the greater the consensus, the more stable and just is the state. There is much evidence that points in the other direction, that the more such a consensus is imposed, the more oppressive and brittle the state becomes (by brittle is meant something strong if used in a fixed and controlled position, but fragile if exposed to unexpected pressures).

'Consensus' is not something to be invoked like spiritual cement to stick something together that would otherwise be broken apart; it is, on the contrary, a quality which arises to ease the continued coexistence of those who have already been living together. It is not prior to the experience of a political community; it is a product of that experience, and therefore cannot meaningfully be taught until a person understands, however generally and simply, the actual political problems and controversies of his community. Certainly 'the parliamentary system' and the 'constitution' are values but they must not be treated as if they are primary values – like justice, rights, equality, freedom, love, truth, welfare, fraternity, compassion and responsibility: they are secondary values or procedural values, valuable in so far as they help enhance and realize primary values in many different forms and circumstances. If all that is taught is the need to respect the secondary or procedural values of 'our parliament' or 'the constitution' as if they were primary values, ends in themselves rather than as means to democratic ends, then naturally any people of an individual or civic spirit will suspect, as Marxists put it, that these concepts are masking hidden values – and because hidden, oppressive and bad. I have found it difficult to convince some students that the concealed values that they seek to unmask can, in fact, often be innocuous, sometimes in themselves even good values. The appearance of deliberate indoctrination, that can easily be created by going on and on about the rules and procedures of parliament and the constitution, is as often bad teaching as it is covert politics.

I find the case for teaching politics in schools, as part of a general and liberal education, an obvious one. But it must be taught realistically, otherwise it can create either more cynicism or more disillusion than would have been created by its absence. By realistically I mean teaching which will encourage a growing and more detailed awareness that constitutions and the particular form of a parliament are devices for conciliating, sometimes resolving but as often merely containing real, and often basic, conflicts of interest and values. To say differences of opinion is too weak an expression. Conflict does not necessarily imply violence, not by any means: it is perhaps more often a matter of persuasion and of ballot; but conflicts of economic and social interest can easily turn violent, if political will and skill fail. This is precisely why a political education is so important, and why it must inform the pupil, in an increasingly complex manner up through the age groups and ability levels, what the basic conflicts in our society are. Only then can the pupil grow to understand the importance of mere procedural rules. He is indeed a fool if he takes it for granted that the constitution is a good thing. He will want to know – if he is the kind of person whom free societies need as citizens, not simply subjects – how it actually works and which problems it resolves, stifles or ignores. The difficulty about civic education is that it must be aimed at creating citizens. If we want a passive population, leave well alone.

Some are tempted to argue that we face disaster and a breakdown of the parliamentary system unless we do something urgently about civic education. Personally, I am not one who can, in Great Britain, beat these alarm drums with much conviction. 'Beware Breakdown' is a stirring melody, but someone at the other end of the drum can also beat out in perfect harmony a revolutionary tattoo: the system is breaking down anyway, so just hurry down to the pot cellars and sit and wait. In some ways I wish I could beat the drum, it might stir some energy somewhere. But I notice that people who do beat the drum at whichever end seldom seem to act accordingly. The leaders of the Festival of Light [among them Lord Longford] and the editors of *Oz* [heroic 1960s hippy types] were each as theatrical as the other. What is far more likely than breakdown is a gradual decay of civic spirit in Britain. I do not fear growth in the numbers of extremists of either Left or Right so much as a retreat into the immediate home and the materialistic consumer-self, literally a growing selfishness, seediness, second-ratedness, lack of energy, indifference and a could-not-care-lessitude; a growth of permissiveness, in its true sense, a sense that should affront any radical as much as any author of a Black Paper on education [or the Campaign for Real Education]: that of simply not caring to draw any moral distinctions any more, a kind of liberalism gone soft, as if it is as wrong to persuade as to coerce; a care only for material excitements, no interest in caring for others. Such permissiveness is, of course, not really a socialist or a radical ethic, but an aristocratic one, not even anarchist in logical outcome but nihilistic; and it is propagated far more effectively by admen, trying to break down the remnants of a sensible middle-class and puritan prejudice against extravagance than it is by the underground press or by, as some profess to believe, aberrant teachers. The opposite of an oppressive society is not a permissive society, but a tolerant society, not the absence of values, but a plurality of values. It is in this context that a genuine citizenship education is needed. In any case, if it were true that we are faced with an impending breakdown of society, schools would be unequipped to arrest it: solutions could only lie in the sphere of public action by political parties and governments.

It is as dangerous to expect too much from civic education, indeed from education generally, as it is to expect too little. But if the real fear is decay, decline and purposelessness, then an enhanced civic education, both more of it and with heightened standards among its teachers, has a crucial role to play. The case for political education is obvious: to learn about politics as one should learn about anything important; to equip an individual better to protect and extend their rights; to give to society as a whole that greater strength and flexibility that comes from voluntary participation rather than from coerced or bribed compliance; and to create or convey that experience of respectful disapproval of other viewpoints which is the basis of toleration which is, in turn, the condition of freedom (Crick, 1971).

How then, in general, should we teach? I have already argued for greater realism and for beginning with a tale drawn from current affairs and contemporary history. The subjects of political dispute must first be identified rather than constitutional rules and parliamentary procedure. The horse really must precede the cart if we are to go anywhere. Any politician knows this; it makes sense. But any politician will doubt the objectivity of any teacher. Your aims are fine, he may say, but are they in fact possible? Does not the teaching of issues degenerate into attempted indoctrination, might not the alternative be neither? We have doubts about churches relying on schools for the teaching of religion, and so do churches. Could not political parties and the media look after civic education better than the school? [And some fatuously say 'the home', which is sometimes the problem and usually an arena of silence about rather than discussion of political and social issues.]

This is not to deny that there can be problems. And some of us at all levels of education could at times brush up our professional standards. Certainly I will defend that certain lecturer's right to his own political opinions (although certainly not to the death); but I would seek to persuade him not to be so self-indulgent and exploitative of his position; and I probably would not promote him for he sounds to me like a thoroughly bad teacher. It is all very well for him to go on and on about the dangers of authority in general; but it would help if he was more aware of his own and if he recognized that no society can flourish without some authority. The question is not one of authority as such, but of the use and abuse of authority. The abuse of authority occurs precisely when a person or institution goes beyond their competence in fulfilling the function for which they should be given respect, attention and a limited obedience, as the case may be, into laying down the law about things irrelevant to their subject – however important. I myself, for instance, claim or gracefully acknowledge some authority as a teacher of politics. I notice that people turn up voluntarily when I come to speak, usually remain, and treat me, happily not always with perfect respect, but at least with reasonable attentiveness and a substantial lack of open interruption. I am reasonably expert as a political theorist in conveying the plausibility of different political doctrines or policies, in identifying basic problems and in analysing what price has to be paid for pursuing one policy rather than another, and when contradictions are practical rather than formal. Opinions of other authorities may differ, but I notice a fair number of us who are treated as authorities none the less. I can go further than that: I may also have a more modest and tentative authority as a political philosopher in analysing what kind of principles, rules or standards can be sensibly invoked in debate about political differences (which has nothing to do with the differences themselves). *But as a teacher I have no kind of authority whatever* in propagating political doctrines, to lay down the law about what should be done. I may say so, I do frequently say so; but in doing so I either abuse my authority in speaking thus on formal or academic occasions, or more often, my authority is simply not relevant and is, I hope, ignored. [Usually I am self-conscious enough to wrap any advocacy in humour, irony or obvious exaggeration.]

Three obvious types of flagrant bias exist. The socialist of 57 varieties (or 58 counting myself) who goes on and on teaching that 'it is all a racket' and 'what should be done about it' is only the most famous case, and somewhat unfairly so, for there is also the [old Tory] Conservative who avoids all discussion of political problems, sticks to the constitution but builds into its alleged rules all his or her own prejudices about the virtues of traditional order and the dangers of change. Similarly, there is the Liberal who teaches that institutional and electoral reform alone will solve all things, and in the name of civics creates a unique and deadly brew of disillusionment with the past coupled with a guarantee of perpetual frustration in the future. And, of course, we all mean so well. I do not, in fact, believe that flagrant bias is very common [as some newspapers delight to suggest – pot calling the kettle black on a cosmic scale]; but the indulgent or the unselfcritical few discredit the sensible, professional many.

Among those who admit that there is a problem of flagrant bias, two kinds of response have been the most usual. The first I call the Swinburnian or the exhortatory school. Like Swinburne they take the view that if one needs must sin, and one needs must, then sin openly, grandly and 'honestly'. Bias cannot be avoided (or a few hardy souls are simply sure that they are right and others are wrong); in which case, air it openly! To be openly and passionately 'something-or-other-istic' will stimulate one's hearers into taking the subject seriously, into forming their own views or counter-attack. [The Socratic and the Marxist dialectic meet and mate.] This is how Harold Laski used to teach. And it was wonderful to hear him: such a completely dedicated, biased but tolerant man. He took great delight in occasionally being contradicted even during a lecture; even in those far-off legendary, disciplined days before the invention of the 1960s, Mr Wedgwood Benn and spontaneous participation. Laski needed to delight in interventions, for they alone could vindicate this alleged teaching method. Few students were, in fact, stirred to an equally passionate and informed opposition; those who did not like it, simply switched off, were more sceptical about authority than ever. For to them he became authority and its typical abuse; and they turned in the expected answers in the exams. (There was parrot Laski at the London School of Economics just as there was to be parrot Oakshott within two years of Laski's death.) If university students did not respond by creative antagonism to this one-way dialectic, how much less likely that those school pupils will? They will either accept or reject not just it, but the whole problem or subject. And a good job too.

I admire the natural, protective scepticism of secondary school children which limits the damage that exhortatory teaching can do in any field of practical morals. [I learnt my scepticism at a church school, not from wicked books.] The trouble is, however, that this scepticism is negative, it prevents disaster (much like our present state of parliamentary politics), but it seems to inhibit the making of real decisions and commitments by the individuals in politics.

The other common response is the constitutional approach, sometimes supplemented by catalogues of pure facts about administration and local government. When I argued against the adequacy of teaching 'the constitution' as a starting point, I did not deny that there are in a clear sense important

43

constitutional rules. But if they should not mean anything to the wise except as a response to the basic political problems of our recent and past history, then how can they be meaningfully and interestingly taught in schools in advance of a knowledge of what our main political problems are and have been? And the particular deadly badge of the constitutional-factual approach is 'the comprehensive textbook'. For once the bit is riveted to the teeth, anything can be tackled and reduced to the same apolitical flatness. What have been the main proposals for constitutional reform?, asks an A level board, which is then tackled in exactly the same prepackaged spirit as 'What are the duties of the Speaker of the House of Commons?' [or whatever, whenever, so long as purely factual]. By contrast, 'Why did demands for parliamentary reform arise in the 1960s?' is a much more interesting, stretching and political question, whereas a full answer to the speaker question could only and should only be looked up in a reference book.

In reducing politics to quasi-legal fact, or in avoiding it altogether in schools and colleges, who knows whether bad teaching, bad syllabuses or ultra-caution is most to blame? But if there are local politicians who are nervous of schools and colleges teaching politics and citizenship, surely their sense of realism could lead them to see that probably more harm is done by the constitutional-factual school in boring pupils and making them believe that the real problems are being withheld from them, than can be done even by the excesses of the 'open and honest bias school'. I do not favour that school. I think it is a mistaken theory of education, frequently an irresponsible self-indulgence on the part of the teacher or lecturer, or sometimes just plain incompetence to convey the inwardness of their doctrines. I only speculate that it may at least keep alive a sense of citizenship and an interest in politics, whereas the former however well-meant makes politicians seem both dull and evasive (which as a type they certainly are not – 'what never?' 'Well, hardly ever', being more often quirky individualists willing to talk very freely, if asked).

44

How then, specifically, should politics be taught? The constitutional and the exhortatory-bias schools have the most spokesmen, but they do not exclude other possibilities. There is an alternative. What I want now very briefly to argue (and to spend some years working out its implications) is not so much novel, as seldom expressed: it is probably the common sense of the average good teacher. Start from the premiss that in politics and in morals there is no way of proving what is best. But there are ways of arguing reasonably, which at least exclude some possibilities. Everything that is possible is not therefore equally desirable. At the end of the day, however, people will differ; but it is likely that they will differ less violently the more they know about the lives, motives and beliefs of those they differ from. Prejudice does not always vanish with greater knowledge, but it is usually diminished and made more containable; and I personally do believe that there are genuine differences of values, not simply prejudices.

While it is not possible to say objectively what should be done, it is easily possible to be reasonably objective and truthful in our use of evidence in political and moral argument, even to reach broad agreement among antagonists as to what counts as evidence relevant to a dispute. Political education is not unlike a judicial process in the Common Law tradition. Evidence is presented not by a judge or officials but by advocates. But the evidence and the advocacy have to be of a kind that would convince a judge or jury. The advocate has no business being on his feet if he has not a case; but he is incompetent to present his case if he cannot handle evidence objectively. The analogy is not exact. It is relevant to the relationship between bias and objectivity rather than to the structure of authority in courts or schools. I am not saying that the teacher should simply be neutral, judging and conducting teaching always or often by debated and exploratory discussion. Even if he were to try this, he would have to teach the young the reasonable cases that provide justifications for their prejudices. The teacher has, certainly in the early stages, to be judge, prosecution and defence rolled into one. But just as he has to show what is evidence, he also has to show how it can reasonably be interpreted differently – and in typical patterns, that are often conservative, liberal or socialist. And not just the concepts they hold, but how they use them. The teacher's own view (for I think it likely that he or she will have one, or else be a very dull teacher), will be relevant at the end of the process, if the pupils ask. It would be an evasion not to answer truthfully, especially if silence fortified the myth of objectivity about values. But it is impertinent and irrelevant to put the question too soon. After showing how the same facts get interpreted in typically different ways, then my own view falling into place and proportion can do less direct harm than others may fear or less direct good than I may rashly hope. But the class may end up thinking for themselves a little bit more and with better knowledge of consequences. [Thinking about probable consequences plays a large part in constituting responsibility.]

Where to start? As a political theorist, I can offer some amateur but common-sense suggestions. Educationalists in Britain, unlike in Germany and America, for instance, have given the subject little thought. I see a strong case for starting with the issues of the moment (of course, one keeps on coming back to them at every level), and of giving an accurate and simplified account of what they are. At the next stage, ability level or class year, go on to set these problems and disputes in their historical context (the dead ground of recent history, ignored by most of the books). One must start somewhere. 'What was the effect of the Second World War on British politics?' 'What did Labour do after it and why?' 'How did the Conservatives come back and what changes did they bring about?' [Update these examples, indeed.] This may worry the historian (too near) and disappoint some of the more lively teachers of politics (too far). But I cannot see how one can create any understanding of both the objectives and the limitations of British politics (for one must always trim between the disinterest that comes from there being no objectives and the disillusion that comes from those objectives being unrealistic) unless topical problems are set in a fairly broad historical context, however thin the detail has to be for whatever attainment level. (We are talking, please, of political education for all, not of A level and pre-university.)

Then at the next stage, there is a double need. By then there should be enough general knowledge of political issues and problems to see how the institutions of government, parliament and party deal with them – which leads one into some of the more important conventions of the constitution. At the same time one must attempt to formalize how and why the parties have differed through the events of the first two stages, that is to elaborate an understanding of them as bodies of doctrine which involve not merely different objectives but also different ways of perceiving political problems, sometimes even different views as to what are problems. This dual task sounds a tall order, especially if one were talking of a one-year rather than a two-year process. [How low one set one's sights twenty years ago!] But I would argue that it is so important to relate institutions to ideas, to show that the one necessarily involves the other, and that the two final stages in a political education must be taken together, however big a sacrifice is needed of content and coverage. So much more important that children learn to think politically than that they can define the powers of the District Auditor or name all the parliamentary regimes of the world. [Critical thinking is a transferable skill.]

Underlying each level the teacher should have clearly worked out some short list of the basic political concepts, such as power, authority and liberty, etc., whose usage his examples should illustrate. I do not think that they can usefully be taught and discussed directly and explicitly except at a really advanced level. Always start with problems, but use them to illustrate concepts; otherwise realism is wholly directionless and impressionistic. I am not quite saying, as do some educationalists, that every subject can be reduced to a limited vocabulary of concepts. There are special difficulties in politics as in other moral and humanistic subjects. But some simplifications are justifiable for heuristic purposes. Better almost any framework than none, or the pretence that there is none, which merely means that the concepts are implicit, unconscious or masked.

At every level, however, the main task is to create empathy, to create an understanding of the plausibility of the differing viewpoints that the student is likely to encounter in his life, and how these viewpoints do not merely define objectives, but define problems too. That 'willing suspension of disbelief' of which Coleridge spoke as constituting poetic faith is called for every day in politics and in political education. Political thought does not call on us to love our adversaries, or anything as extreme or as way-out as that, but simply that we understand them; perhaps in order to oppose them more effectively. Political thinking may create more mutual respect, but it will not obliterate differences. It is lack of this empathy that often worries me about university students and some teachers. Personally I hold some strong views; but although a democratic Socialist, I am obsessed with the plausibility, for instance, of Conservatism. I teach that Conservatism is a doctrine of government: it says that those who govern best are those who are most experienced, thus the rise and fall of societies is to be explained by the character of the governing class. And it is a doctrine of change: that gradual change is always best, to respond flexibly to events (of which so much cannot be controlled anyway), rather than to try to shape them. Hence the importance of tradition. [This was before, of course, Thatcher purged the old Tories in favour of market liberalism.] Many other versions could be advanced, but I think my account would be regarded as fair in the sense that many Conservatives would accept it. And I 'teach it' not just as a doctrine to be described but as a highly plausible theory of history and politics to be used. Certainly Conservatives have succeeded in governing Britain more often than not since the great Reform Bill of 1867, and certainly most situations are to be understood in terms of historical antecedents, rather than as acts of deliberate will. The Liberal would say that societies rise, fall, prosper or decay because of individual invention and initiative: he sees politics in terms of the rights and capabilities of individuals. The Socialist sees the basis of society as the relationship of man-as-worker to methods of production; individuals are defined and limited by their position in social groups, and ultimately groups formed by co-operation will prove more strong and productive than groups formed by economic competition.

Now, of course, that is a foolishly oversimplified model [and arguably sadly dated]. There are many subcategories; and there are even political doctrines that cut across such party ideologies – such as nationalism and faith in technicians. I only report that I have found this simple triad reasonably fruitful to use, and think that it can be used at any level. Perhaps at the very simplest level one can say that the Conservative thinks that the distribution of power and goods would not be as it is without good reason; the Liberal thinks that distribution could and should be made more fair in relation to ability; and the Socialist thinks that distribution could and should be made radically more equal. But I also report a lack even in some first-year university students of any ability to express the plausibility of persuasions other than their own, either as doctrines of action or explanatory theories of society. Something of this nature could be done earlier. At present there is more need to stimulate knowledge and empathy rather than mere self-expression. That is the challenge to teachers. And it can be assessed.

Thus I would reject both the value-free and the honest bias approach to political education. Quite simply, it is impossible to be value-free and attempts to achieve this blissful state of moral suspension involve high degrees of either boredom or self-deception. At the end of the day after, but only after, some empathy has been stimulated for the beliefs and motivations of the many political doctrines and moral codes that coexist in our society, the recognition of bias can even be helpful in stimulating a concern for active citizenship. Biased opinions by themselves do no harm: what matters is *how* we hold our opinions, whether tolerantly, reasonably, with

49

respect for those of others, and with some thought of the consequences of acting on beliefs, after considering contrary evidence.

Simple bias, then, is all but unavoidable and is no more harmful than tastes for this or that food, drink, music or fashion when not pushed to excess at the expense of reasoned judgement about everything else – like a child calling foods that it simply does not like, 'horrid!' and 'nasty, nasty'. What is excess? When one's taste or partisanship leads one not merely to run down a contrary position, but also to give an almost wholly unrecognizable account of it. Simple bias is when one's prejudices are clear but one's judgement is reasonable; and gross bias is when one's perceptions of what one is prejudiced against are so distorted as to be useless in dealing with those problems or people in a political manner. Gross bias, in other words, destroys the accuracy of the perceptions; as well as being completely unacceptable to the other as a description of themselves.

The proof of the pudding is ever in the eating. Assessment, that is examination, of the style of teaching about politics that we are advocating will tell one far more than the memory tests of the powers of the Prime Minister and the stages of a Public Bill. Examinations should assess whether students can argue a case for and against a proposal, whether they could identify what party or pressure group adheres to which of some stated policies, and how different political adherents would react to a stated problem. The practical answer to fears of bias is for the aims of the course to be clearly assessable: will it have increased their knowledge of real political issues and of other people's reactions to them?

After informative and empathetic teaching can come commitment, for the pupil, or the 'unmasking' of the teacher; but only after, not before. The temporal order is crucial. Syllabuses need changing and making more realistic to ensure this, but professional standards may need tightening as well. Political teaching should at least be open. The 'honest bias' school are right in this, at least. The teacher is a whole person, just as is the party member or the school governor or the local councillor. In civilized states we are used to playing different roles at different times, but rarely, only in the most special cases, does one role utterly exclude another. Some bias and some confusion of roles cannot be avoided, so to go to drastic extremes to avoid them is usually to create a cure far worse than a mild disease. We may sometimes need more self-restraint, but seldom sterilizing. If there is a flagrant bias, it would matter far less if the syllabuses were more realistic and the teaching more knowledgeably empathetic. Good teaching is not entirely a matter of honesty and dedication: it is also a matter of greater professionalism. Colleges and Institutes of Education should give up their economic or nervous habit of treating politics as, at best, a subsidiary part of another discipline; far more specialist appointments are needed, and creative work on curriculum development. But, of course, in the end it does all depend on the teacher. And if teachers cannot be trusted to teach politics, however professionally, they ultimately should not be trusted to teach geometry – for one man who taught me, I well remember, taught geometry as a proof that the universe was designed by God and another saw it as a self-evident demonstration of materialism. Both were good teachers.

Postscript

Two important books on indoctrination appeared at about the same time as I wrote and published the first version of this essay: *Concepts of Indoctrination: Philosophical Essays*, edited by I. A. Snook and *Indoctrination and Education*, by I. A. Snook (both from Routledge and Kegan Paul, 1972). I added a review of them (which first appeared in *Teaching Politics*, May 1974 [now unhappily renamed and reoriented as *Talking Politics* and aimed almost entirely at A level and GCSE exam preparation].

As Professor Peter Richards said, the general editor of the International Library of the Philosophy of Education in which series Dr Snook's anthology is part, there is a growing interest in the philosophy of education among students of philosophy as well as amongst those specifically and practically concerned with education. He may seem, with some excuse, to be blowing his own trumpet – which I have always thought more modest than inducing others to do it for one. Philosophers in the analytical tradition of philosophy are not necessarily becoming more concerned with ethics, education and politics, but they are showing welcome signs of boredom with the world of purely invented examples. They are taking the trouble to inform themselves a little about some other disciplines or problem areas which raise interesting, part philosophical and part practical questions.

'Indoctrination' is one of the most interesting and important of these. Nowadays there is a widespread suspicion that if anyone talks about religious, moral or political education, some form of indoctrination is being suggested and that indoctrination is bad. But not so long ago it was taken for granted that indoctrination should take place in these areas: the main debate was whether it should be done directly or indirectly. Have our attitudes changed or has there been a shift of meaning in the concept? I think it fairly clear that our attitudes have changed. We do think it wrong that religious or political belief should be imposed on children. And also our empirical beliefs have changed: most social scientists are now sceptical that general adherence to a clearly defined moral doctrine is necessary for the preservation of social order. This was once regarded as axiomatic. We are aware that politically organized societies can and commonly do contain a plurality of value-systems within them. If 'consensus' has any meaning – and I for one am sceptical of its use as an explanation of how order is maintained; especially as it is then so often treated, in the next breath, as a consequence of order rather than a cause – if consensus has any meaning, it is plainly at a level of abstraction concerned with norms, rules and *procedures*, not with the *substantive content* of moral and political doctrines.

We now all seem suspiciously unanimous against indoctrination. The traditionalist fears that any political education will necessarily involve indoctrination; and the revolutionary generously hints that the whole educational system is indoctrinatory. So perhaps the usage and meaning has also shifted as well as our attitudes to it, if all feel against it: 'You are a hack teacher, he indoctrinates, I am ideologically correct.' The two books cover much the same ground, even reach much the same qualified, tentative yet clear enough conclusions, but they are at different levels of complexity. The symposium gathers in all the most important articles on the problem of recent years, except for two, constantly referred to, which were not available because of copyright difficulties: John Wilson's 'Indoctrination and Education' and R. M. Hare's 'Adolescents into Adults', both of which can be found in T. H. B. Hollins (ed.) *Aims in Education: The Philosophical Approach* (Manchester University Press, 1964). The controversy about the actual meaning or the most useful meaning of the concept centres on method, content and intentions. Some hold that any beliefs can be indoctrinated, others argue that indoctrination can only properly be used of false or doubtful beliefs, and others that only beliefs in the elaborated forms that it is sensible to call 'doctrines' can be indoctrinated (that is, it refers to something both systematic and important). Difficulties abound. If method is the key, must it work? Suppose my statistical sample is deliberately biased, and yet none the less I reach a true result; or is all unmethodical teaching (as the sociology of education adherents so often suggest) indoctrinatory – in the sense of uncritically relaying accepted social values? If content is the crux, then falsehood should reign; yet surely very often precisely what we mean by indoctrination is when *the truth* is thrust on us. And the content could be false, expertly indoctrinated and yet somehow not believed: the effort proves counter-productive. Suppose a man teaches a false scientific belief, say that the earth is flat or is dogmatic that the universe must be finite. If contrary evidence is not available, it would be foolish to call such teaching of received truths indoctrination. The evidence may be available in principle, although it is necessary to remember whose practical dilemma we are considering: a schoolteacher is not a research scientist. Strictly speaking he or she cannot be held responsible for whether such things are true or false, only responsible for whether the sources he uses can reasonably be regarded as authoritative. All authorities – to anticipate – must be questioned, none must be above explaining *why* they may be treated as authoritative; but the teacher himself cannot replace authorities. [And the suppression of well-known contrary evidence is certainly indoctrination.]

The twelve essays are nearly all of high standard and very stretching. I find the contributions by Anthony Flew, R. F. Atkinson and John Wilson particularly interesting. But it is fair to warn that they are more likely to interest philosophers in some aspects of education than to be readily grasped by any but the most able BEd students in the colleges of education. So it was a most excellent idea to bring out at the same time in the justly famed Students Library of Education a short and truly elementary book covering the same ground. Snook's own book should be read and pondered by every teacher of politics. And it has an excellent bibliography.

He lucidly expounds the distinctions he made in his own important essay in the anthology. *Cases of clear indoctrination*: (a) teaching an ideology as if it were the only possible one with a claim to rationality; (b) teaching, as if they are certain, propositions the teacher knows to be uncertain; and (c) teaching propositions which are false and known by the teacher to be false. *Cases which seem like indoctrination*, but which are not since they are unavoidable in any possible society: (a) teaching young children what is conventionally regarded as correct behaviour (i.e. there will always be some conventions, and it is not indoctrination if taught as conventions and not truths – as John Wilson argues, children need to know what various moral codes are); (b) teaching facts by rote (e.g. the tables – whichever way round); and (c) unconsciously influencing the child in certain directions (although once you realize you are having such and such a side effect, it could be indoctrinatory not to attempt to reduce or change the effect).

Problematic cases: (a) inculcating doctrines believed by the teacher to be certain but which are substantially disputed (problematic because often the teacher is not to know whether the textbook writer is just a lazy old dog or a deliberate reactionary refusing to present newer, alternative explanations); and (b) teaching any subject, he concludes, for example even chemistry, without due concern for critical understanding. To Snook understanding, rationality and evidence are what divides education from indoctrination. In the small book he sums up his contentions:

> I have argued that the indoctrinator intends the pupil to believe 'P' regardless of the evidence. In full blown cases on intention, this captures very well the difference between the indoctrinator and the educator. For the educator, the beliefs are always secondary to the evidence: he wants his students to end up with whatever beliefs the evidence demands. He is concerned with methods of assessing data, standards of accuracy, and validity of reasoning. The answers are subsidiary to the methods of gaining answers. The indoctrinator, however, is typically more concerned with the imparting of beliefs ... it is the evidence that is of subsidiary importance.

Thus, Snook argues convincingly that indoctrination is teaching something in such a manner that it is believed regardless of evidence. Evidence is, of course, often not scorned; he points out that the real doctrinaire may rehearse his classes in the most elaborate 'proofs' by rote. My only criticism of Snook's excellent analysis is that he does not really explore procedures for discriminating between such 'proofs' and those probabilities which carry with them the inner worm of doubt, true civilized scepticism and tolerance. [The passions stirred by the opponents of GM foods are an interesting topical example, or the evidence offered by proponents of alternative medicine.] Here I find John Wilson's work in moral education very helpful. I would want to put to Snook that in moral and political education there is usually a fairly limited stock of recognized or seemingly practical alternative viewpoints and explanations. Wilson holds that the pupil must be made aware of the range of these, indeed if he or she is lacking in empathy for them and cannot understand how a sensible person can possibly be a Conservative or a Socialist or whatever, then the pupil must be worked upon by the teacher – with techniques perhaps very much like those of the indoctrinator, except that the object is tolerance and understanding and not a preconceived belief. [Put it another way, pupils need to be warned what they will encounter in the adult world.]

A further question at a deeper level raises itself in both books. Can indoctrination ever be justified? Surely the democratization of Germany after the Second World War? or what about aversion therapy? Should we not indoctrinate democracy? Oddly, this question is never quite met head on. The readings lack a political philosopher, and Snook, like John Wilson and Jacob Bruner, despite many a glancing side reference to politics, somehow avoids the most difficult and important field of applied ethics (at least to Aristotle and the whole speculative tradition of reason and nature that followed from him), the political way itself (the middle way of creative compromise). I think the formal answer is fairly simple. To indoctrinate democracy is a contradiction in terms if 'democracy' is really democratic. This is a different question from whether or not constraint is needed to introduce political education (of a quite new kind) into German schools or more generally to keep any children in school at all (an assumption that some mystical-technocrats would now challenge). But a democratic political process, a genuine political education and a scientific method that attempts to falsify its own hypotheses as its only view of how to advance truth or truths (and which can while proceeding through doubt and scepticism yet generalize with such astounding accuracy), these have much in common. Why do we so often hesitate to say? [If this sounds Popperian, it is.]

56

I find it odd to reflect that in the fields where people are most worried about indoctrination, that is religious and political education, there is already a plurality of viewpoints which should actually make the task of the teacher easier – once the teacher sees that the task is not to avoid any discussion of beliefs, but is to explain and understand the differences between the common beliefs that there are. It is much more difficult to avoid indoctrination, believing that one is teaching the truth and nothing but the truth, in fields some of whose occupants give themselves such (pseudo) scientific airs, like psychology and economics. But full-blown indoctrination and gross bias is probably a more rare thing [among teachers] than most suppose – simple bias is the more common and everyday lesser problem. The far more serious arena of bias, deliberate and distorting bias at that, is found every day when one opens almost any newspaper, but oddly that seems to worry people less.

4 Political literacy

This paper was written in collaboration with Ian Lister. Some preceeding paragraphs are added from 'An Explanatory Paper', both from the Hansard Society's Programme for Political Education which we jointly headed. (Crick and Porter, 1978)

The Hansard Society working party identified three possible aims for political education which are often seen as alternatives, and as mutually exclusive:

(a) The purely and properly conserving level of knowing how our present system of government works, and knowing the beliefs that are thought to be part of it.
(b) The liberal or participatory level of development of the knowledge, attitudes and skills necessary for an active citizenship.
(c) Beyond both of these there lies the more contentious area of considering possible changes of direction of government or of alternative systems.

We said that the last was, indeed, a perfectly proper area of educational concern, capable of treatment without gross bias, but only when taken together with some consideration of the previous two. We are inclined to doubt the alleged stimulating effect of starting the teaching by dealing with extreme or minority rousing viewpoints – as some have argued. The educational justification can be that dealing with this third

59

objective is habituating the pupil to the critical use of partisan sources, such as he will meet in the real world, whereas the second only habituates him to, at the best, conflicts of values or more often simply to following through the implications of his own beliefs. We once suggested that these three different objectives can be seen as a sequence of stages or levels through which a full programme for political education in secondary schools should move, but we now think that there is no necessary sequence of stages or levels so long as all three occur in a full programme for political education. To be relevant and to arouse interest, the experience of many teachers suggests, to begin by considering alternatives can sometimes stimulate students into appreciating how specific and significant are the ordinary institutions (of the first category) which otherwise they would take completely for granted or regard as banal. However, equally obviously, any prolonged consideration of alternative institutions or societies should only be returned to after facts and opinions about conserving what we have that works well enough, and the opportunities and limits of participation have been considered in some depth. The safest generalization, in other words, is that all three objectives must find their place in a curriculum together and not be taught in isolation or to the exclusion of others.

Right from the beginning, then, we pointed out that theories of the aims of political education are necessarily close to the main doctrines of politics, of conservation, participation and of change. Perhaps it is for this reason that we prefer to see the objective of our whole Programme as to enhance 'political literacy' rather than 'political education'. Strictly speaking, political education could be seen as instrumental: working towards realizing certain preconceived political objectives [as in autocracies and dictatorships]. The politically literate man or woman would be somebody who (however he or she may act in a personal capacity) can appreciate the plausibility of and give some good account of the nature and implications of each of these three doctrines. It is hard, indeed, to see how any account of politics can be plausible which does not draw, in different circumstances and for different purposes, on each of these three theories or doctrines.

So we now discuss the central concept of the project. By political literacy we mean a compound of knowledge, skills and attitudes, to be developed together, each one conditioning the other two. To meet the needs of the vast majority of young people, basic political literacy means a practical understanding of concepts drawn from everyday life and language. To have achieved political literacy is to have learnt what the main political disputes are about, what beliefs the main contestants have of them, how they are likely to affect you and me. It also means that we are likely to be predisposed to try to do something about the issue in question in a manner which is at once effective and respectful of the sincerity of other people and what they believe.

The paper emphasizes that we do not mean something only attained in one way. We are not postulating some universal role or model. There are alternative ways of attaining it as of attaining any skill. But there are common elements which exemplify and typify politically literate persons, what they know, their attitude to what they know and their skill in using what they know.

What kinds of knowledge would a politically literate person possess? (i) The basic information about the issue: who holds the power; where the money comes from; how the institution in question works. (This may apply to Parliament, a committee of the County Council, a factory, a school, a trade union, a voluntary body, a club or even family.) (ii) How to be actively involved using the above knowledge and understanding the nature of the issue. (iii) How to estimate the most effective way of resolving the issue. (iv) How to recognize how well policy objectives have been achieved when the issue is settled. (v) How to comprehend the viewpoints of other people and their justifications for their actions, and always expect to offer justifications oneself.

Such knowledge is used at different levels by different

people. Someone who is highly politically literate will possess the ability to apply sophisticated political concepts. He is also aware of what he does not know, but he knows where that knowledge can be obtained. Basic political literacy for a majority means grasping concepts which grow out of situations which lie within everybody's personal experience.

What are the attitudes of a politically literate person? These must of necessity vary. It is no part of this project to expect that all the values of Western European liberalism will be taken for granted or can be applicable everywhere. What we have inherited as part of our tradition must be subject to criticism and sometimes scepticism. There is in our view no correct attitude to be inculcated as part of political literacy; nevertheless, attitudes will inevitably be adopted, and they will be based consciously or unconsciously on values. One of us identifies 'freedom', 'toleration', 'fairness', 'respect for truth' and 'respect for reasoning' as what he calls 'procedural values': values which are presupposed in political literacy.

What skills would a politically literate person possess? The politically literate person is not merely an informed spectator: he or she is someone capable of active participation and communication, or of a positive and reasoned refusal to participate. At the same time the politically literate person, while tolerating the views of others, is capable of thinking in terms of change and of methods of achieving change. We recognize that the chief difficulty lying in the way of educating for political literacy is not that this might encourage bias on the part of students or indoctrination on the part of teachers, but that it should inevitably and rightly encourage action. We are confident that political action is worthy of encouragement if it is based on knowledge and understanding. Knowledge and understanding cover not only the facts which go to make up the conflict, but the views of the disputants. Empathy with different viewpoints is greatly to be encouraged. All of this is summed up in what has become known as the 'Political Literacy Tree', reproduced below (p. 71).

Finally we stress that the media, not the school, inevitably supply much of the information about politics that a person needs; the role of the school is to help pupils handle this information in a critical way, and to help them to form their own opinions, to appreciate those of others and to give them the will and the means to participate in an effective and responsible manner. We assume that, as part of a general education, pupils acquire some general knowledge of the kind of society in which they live, its people, its history, its beliefs and the broad economic and geographical factors that define and limit that society.

So far we have specified the concept only in very general terms. Now to be more specific. But in being more specific, we must make clear that the concept then appears as a cultural ideal. For most people it is a goal to be achieved, not a summary of experience. Some who by our definition may be politically illiterate can be politically *effective*, but that is not quite the same thing: unconscious habits can sometimes make one politically effective, as may in other circumstances fanatical intensity. Or a passive and deferential population, who think of themselves as good subjects and not active citizens, or who do not think of politics at all, may for some purposes pose few problems to the carrying on of government. But 'political literacy' involves both some conscious understanding of what one is about in a given situation, some flexibility and some capacity for action.

All actions affect others, however, so one needs to be aware of what effects actions are likely to have, and then also to be able to justify them. Some consistency, both in explaining possible consequences and in justifications, must be assumed. Hence to that extent, but to that extent alone, a politically literate person will show some consistency and subtlety in the use of political concepts. But the concepts are likely to be drawn from everyday life and language: a politically literate person may be quite innocent of the more technical vocabulary of the social sciences. We can certainly conceive, as it were, an 'advanced literacy' derived from the social sciences, which would put far more stress on genuine explanation

63

rather than on practical understanding; but this is not our primary concern, for it is not relevant to the needs of the majority of young people in education.

A politically literate person will know what the main issues are in contemporary politics as he himself is affected, and will know how to set about informing himself further about the main arguments employed and how to criticize the relevance or worth of the evidence on which they are based; and he will need as much, but no more, knowledge of institutional structure as he needs to understand the issues and the plausibility of rival policies. A politically literate person will then know what the main political disputes are about; what beliefs the main contestants have of them; how they are likely to affect him, and he will have a predisposition to try to do something about it in a manner at once effective and respectful of the sincerity of others.

Sources of the political

Before going further, however, we must pause to reiterate that underlying any theory of political education and any ideal of political literacy, there must be a theory of politics. Our theory of politics is much broader than many conventional views of politics – broader in two ways.

First, it stresses that politics is inevitably concerned with conflicts of interests and ideals, so an understanding of politics must begin with an understanding of the conflicts that there are and of the reasons and interests of the contestants; it cannot be content with preconceptions of constitutional order or of a necessary consensus. A politically literate person will not hope to resolve all such differences, or difficulties at once; but he perceives their very existence as politics. Second, it stresses the differential distribution of power there is in any society and the differential access to resources. Hence we are concentrating on a whole dimension of human experience which we characterize as political (much as Graeme Moodie has said that a politically literate person would have 'the ability to recognize the political dimensions of any human situations').

Where do we find examples of the political? We find them (i) in the speeches and behaviour of professional politicians and political activists; (ii) in the writings and teaching of political scientists; and (iii) in observing and experiencing what we may call the politics of everyday life – in the family, the locality, educational institutions, clubs and societies and in informal groups of all kinds.

For ordinary people only the third category necessarily involves them in participation. The first two categories involve extraordinarily few people. But one of the aims of political education in general (particularly of this project) is to open up access for majorities to the kinds of information and skills possessed by professional politicians and professional students of politics.

Types of political literacy
Our immediate problem is that we are now passing from the rhetorical stage, where we have asserted political literacy as an ideal, to the second stage, where we must specify it, see how to assess it and discover educational strategies from promoting it. We have identified political literacy as the key element in the Programme for Political Education, not only because (as we use it) it is a much broader concept than, say, 'political competence' or 'political understanding', but also because we believe that we will be able to assess it in ways which are meaningful to a lot of people; and we believe that, particularly in the areas of information and skills, it is teachable and learnable, that its further specification can provide a framework for developing better curricula at all levels.

Political literacy has the further advantage that, being a condition, there might be alternative ways of attaining it (just as there are alternative ways of learning a language and the social actions with which language is related). No two societies will have the same view of it. It is not an absolute condition (a political danger of 'assessing political literacy' is that simplifiers might label majorities 'politically illiterate and unworthy of active participation in political life'). Rather, political literacy has levels of understanding, minimal and advanced, basic and more sophisticated. Whether there are also critical thresholds, between the two levels, is something that we will need to investigate at a later stage.

So in speaking of a 'politically literate person' we are not postulating some universal role or model: different politically literate persons might have quite a lot of characteristics which vary one from another. However, it is the common elements which exemplify and typify politically literate persons that we are interested in. But before we go on to that, there is one caveat: certain kinds of knowledge might be attributes of a politically literate person (such as, they would know the name of the Prime Minister, or the President of the United States), but such knowledge alone would not be a sufficient condition of political literacy. In a similar fashion, while the possession of such knowledge alone would not be a sufficient indicator of political literacy, the lack of such knowledge would be a likely predictor of a low level of political literacy. Thus, political information tests are often more useful to explore ignorance than knowledge.

What kinds of knowledge?

At the most general level a politically literate person would possess the basic information which is prerequisite to understanding the political dimensions of a given context. Thus, there is a sense in which the necessary knowledge is contextually related (if not narrowly contextually defined). For example, in each parliament, factory, school and family, active participants need to know some basic facts about it; something about the structure of power in the institution, where its money comes from and something of the ways and means in which it works. A politically literate person would not only have a high level of understanding of a given context and situation, but would be able to operate efficiently within that context and situation. This would involve having notions of policy, of policy objectives and an ability to recognize how well policy objectives had been achieved as well as being able to comprehend those of others. Political literacy is not simply an ability to pursue even an enlightened self-interest: it must comprehend the effects on others and their viewpoints, and respond to them morally.

A politically literate person would also know the kinds of knowledge that he or she needed, and did not possess, in a given situation, and how to find them out. Paradoxically, the politically literate person knows what he or she does not know.

A politically literate person would possess a knowledge of those concepts minimally necessary to construct simple conceptual and analytical frameworks. These need not necessarily be – indeed are unlikely to be – concepts drawn from the 'high language of politics' (i.e. the arcane language of professional political scientists), but rather from everyday life – yet used more systematically and precisely than is common. Differential political literacy is possible. The professor of Political Science might be quite lost in the politics of Hull docks, or of a social club. Some clusters of concepts, adequate to understanding and even allowing an active participation in a local situation, might be restricted both in time and space. Only a highly politically literate person would have command of both local and more universal concepts. A programme of political education should be aware of both and be able to relate both to each other; it is likely to move towards the more universal, though perhaps to draw its material and examples from the more local or immediate level.

What kind of attitudes and values?

It would be wrong to define a politically literate person as someone who necessarily shares all values of Western European liberalism. That would be, indeed, a curious updating of the Whig interpretation of history into present-day political education. Such views are to be learned as part of our tradition, but they must themselves be subject to criticism; some scepticism must be part of any citizen and of any worthwhile education; and they must not be universalized without the utmost self-awareness, self-criticism and thought for consequences. However, it is clear, at the least, that there are some kinds of political effectiveness which simply destroy the possibility of other kinds of political literacy. Some biases are compatible with a true knowledge of the motives, beliefs and behaviour of others, some not. Functional political literacy may well be imposed and narrowing. All values are not equal.

Attitudes cannot be ignored. We reject the assumptions of those, whether of Left or Right, who would have only the correct attitudes taught (which narrows political literacy) and the theoretical assumption that all values and attitudes are equally 'socialized' – says one theory – or equally important parts of tradition – says another (and therefore beyond the reach of educational reason). Certainly all values should be interpreted in different social contexts, but some are more conditioned than others – to put the case at its weakest. If we value truth and freedom it is not possible to be free of values, and it is a poor example for a teacher to set out to try to do the impossible in some overelaborate manner.

We assume that the teacher should not seek to influence basic substantive values and that frontal assaults are, in any case, not likely to be successful; but that it is both proper and possible to try to nurture and strengthen certain procedural values. Previously we identified 'freedom, toleration, fairness, respect for truth and for reasoning' as such values. Anyone can see that in real life and politics there are many occasions in which those values may have to be modified, because they can conflict with each other, or conflict with some substantive values such as religion, ethical codes and political doctrines embody. Part of political education is to examine just such conflicts: but this does not affect the primacy of these procedural values within a genuine political education. The objection to them is, indeed, more likely to be that they are vague platitudes rather than indoctrinatory concepts. This we will try to resolve in discussing 'Basic Political Concepts'.

What skills are needed?

The real difficulties of political education are likely to lie not in areas of bias and indoctrination but in its encouragement of action. There are still some who appear to want 'good citizenship' without the trouble of having citizens. The great difference between literacy and political literacy is that literacy can involve only a solitary pursuit, but political literacy involves the action and interaction of groups. It is true that certain relevant skills (such as critical and evaluative skills) are 'intellectual' and, like reading, can be performed by the individual in solitude. However, this itself constitutes a very limited notion of political literacy which would preserve politics as a spectator sport for most people, or would reduce the politically literate person to the under-gardener role voluntarily adopted by so many English philosophers, that is dealing only in second-order activities. (As Sir Edward Boyle has put it: 'The major political differences in our national life are not so much between Government and Opposition as between the Government and everybody else. Governments "do", the rest of us talk.')

The ultimate test of political literacy lies in creating a proclivity to action, not in achieving more theoretical analysis. The politically literate person would be capable of active participation (or positive refusal to participate) and should not be excluded from the opportunity to participate merely because of lack of the prerequisite knowledge and skills. The highly politically literate person should be able to do more than merely imagine alternatives. We are not trying to achieve a condition of ecumenical mutual exhaustion, rather a more vigorous kind of tolerance of real views and real behaviour. The politically literate person must be able to devise strategies for influence and for achieving change. He must see the right means to an end he can justify. And while action certainly does not imply any particular kind of change, it does imply effect on others or change of a sort.

The literacy tree

The 'Political Literacy Diagram' attempts to set out in some detail what is minimally involved in political literacy. The specification may seem formidable, but we think that there is no flinching the fact that the number of relationships to be grasped in political literacy (of beyond a minimal kind) is quite large; that it is dangerous to oversimplify what politics is about; and that a major educational effort is needed. However, as will be clear later, the amount of knowledge demanded can be much smaller than is often thought. The media, not the school, inevitably supply much of the information about politics that a person needs: the role of the school is to help him handle this information in a critical way, to help him form his own opinions, to appreciate those of others, to give him the will and the means to participate effectively and responsibly. Similarly, while we specify that the politically literate person must be able to give reasons and justifications for beliefs and actions and to understand those of others, it would be an advanced literacy indeed that could discuss the criteria for the validity of the judgements. That is political philosophy in a technical sense. The respect for reason we talk of only implies the giving and the demanding of reasons at all. The meaning and the implications of political beliefs, but not their validity, is all we hope to be generally examined in schools.

The fundamental point arises because people are in fact faced with issues and problems of a political nature. Civic need and educational theory go together. The teaching of politics and the learning about politics must arise from issues and experience. We reject the argument that a knowledge of institutions must come first. The politically literate person needs to know about institutions, but only as much as is

70

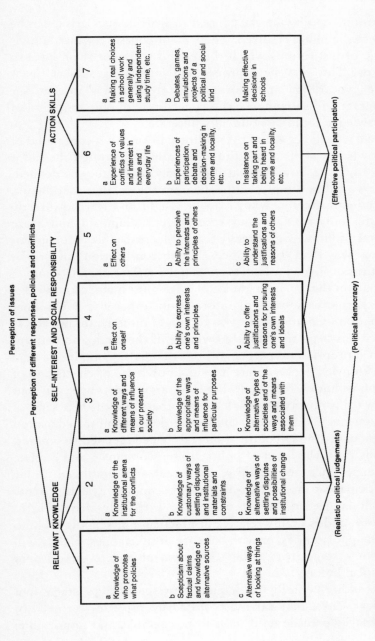

Figure 4.1 The Political Literacy Tree

relevant to knowing the context in which issues arise, can be affected and are resolved. There is, of course, a wider knowledge of institutions which those who work for them have to know. This may be a proper and interesting subject for A level, vocational and university study. But a glance at our diagram will show how easily a person with only that kind of knowledge could be politically illiterate.

We repeat, yet again, that political literacy is a compound of knowledge, skills and attitudes. We have laboured the point already as to how these attitudes may reasonably be defined. But we did not imply, as the diagram shows, that they should be taught directly. What is to be taught and learned directly relates only to skills and knowledge. Columns 1 and 2 are forms of knowledge directly teachable, teachable in a conventional way that, for instance, 'British constitution' or 'British institutions' have often been taught, except that Column 1 stipulates that such taught knowledge must include knowledge of alternative sources of information (otherwise it is indoctrination). Column 3 can also be taught directly, though it less often has been taught: a knowledge of the tactics and strategies appropriate to particular political goals. Columns 4 and 5 are knowledge of a different kind, knowledge of effects and of responsibilities, of what kind of arguments one can put forward to justify some effects on others and of their kind of arguments. This is now commonly done in moral education curricula, although oddly it has rarely been related to politics, though it is the heart of political life. Columns 6 and 7 relate to experience and activity, both real and simulated. Some participation in decision-making in school is essential. How much is needed, we recognize, is extremely debatable in theory, and is highly relative in practice. But schools with no such opportunities, or with derisory or token ones, plainly will at some stage in a child's development negate our idea of political literacy.

Read horizontally the diagram represents stages, stages in a logical sense, that (a) must ordinarily precede (b), and (b) ordinarily precede (c) if (c) is to be effective, and responsible.

These are also possible stages in curriculum development, though we see all this as ordinarily fitting into a very short compass of time. As we have already said, knowledge of alternative forms of political and social organization is a necessary part of a political education, but that it is not the best way to begin – only after conservative factors and participative opportunities have been explored should one begin to think about alternatives. However minimal political literacy, however little time is available for political education, it must involve knowing what the main issues are thought to be. The kind of sources we will suggest (opinion polls, party manifestos and newspapers) are unlikely to come up with more than a half-dozen issues which dominate politics at any given time. But even these are too many to be pursued through the twelve or so operations we suggest. Only one or two would be followed in small modules of politics, but the skills and perceptions that could then be formed or strengthened would have, we suggest, a general applicability: a transferable skill would have been created.

An advanced political literacy may well be defined in terms of (i) an explicit and critical study of this model and its simplifications; (ii) extending it into consideration of alternative forms of political and social organization; (iii) criteria for judgement and justifications and for political obligation and disobedience; and (iv) knowing what political science has to say of relevance to these factors.

Perhaps there is no need to say that in asserting the very great social and educational importance of political literacy, we have tried to narrow the concept down to the specifically political so that it can be integrated with other subjects. Indeed, politics is not an end in itself, but a relationship between or within other things. For these reasons we have not specified what is obvious, that a politically literate person will be numerate and literate, have some general knowledge of the kind of society he or she lives in, its people, history and the broad economic and geographical factors that define and limit us. All this is part of a general education.

So what we offer in the diagram has two direct purposes: (i) as criteria by which it may be possible to assess whether a person is politically literate or a curriculum likely to enhance it; and (ii) as a direct outline or general model of what should be involved in all political education.

For the moment we leave aside the important question of attitudes and values. Our view is clear, that some are to be taught and learned, but none can be taught directly. In the paper that follows, on 'Basic concepts', we will make clear which combination of factors in the diagram relate the most to particular basic 'procedural values' (freedom, toleration, fairness, respect for the truth and for reasoning), and will suggest at what stage each of the suggested elements in a larger but minimal family of political concepts can best be introduced.

5 Basic concepts for political education

This paper, in the Hansard Society's Programme for Political Literacy (Crick and Porter, 1978) followed that on 'Political Literacy' above.

In the last chapter it was suggested that 'a politically literate person would possess a knowledge of those concepts minimally necessary to construct simple conceptual and analytical frameworks'. These need not necessarily be – indeed are unlikely to be – concepts drawn from 'the high language of politics', i.e. the arcane language of professional political scientists, but rather from everyday life – yet employed more systematically and precisely than is usual.

This paper simply suggests one possible set of basic concepts and offers working definitions of them for the teacher to apply to whatever materials he or she is using. Since there is no possibility of final agreement either about which concepts are minimal and which are basic (that is, not a compound of others), this paper is inevitably more personal than some others in the Programme. The Working Party endorse it simply as a useful contribution to discussion rather than as a policy document or as carrying their agreement in every respect.

We perceive and we think in concepts. Concepts are, as it were, the building blocks with which we construct a picture of the external world, including imaginary or hoped-for worlds. So concepts are not true or false, they simply help us to perceive and to communicate. To quote an earlier article of mine which offers a fuller justification of this approach:

> I will argue for a conceptual approach, that is I believe that all education, whether in school or out of school, consists in increasing understanding of language and increasing ability to use it to adjust to external relationships and events, to extend one's range of choice within them and finally to influence them. At all times we have some general image of the world in which we live, some understanding, however tentative, primitive or even false and the slightest degree of education consists in forming explanations of these images or offering generalizations, however simple, about alternative images or modifications of early ones, with some argument, some appeal to evidence. The images are composed of concepts. Willy-nilly, we begin with concepts and we try to sharpen them, to extend their meanings, to see links between them and then to go on to invent or accept special sets of concepts for new problems   (Crick, 1974)

By a 'conceptual approach' I do not mean that concepts themselves should be taught directly. The approach is for the teacher, not necessarily the class; it is an underpinning of curricula, not an outline curriculum. A 'conceptual approach' only accentuates the positive, that we think and perceive in concepts, and eliminates the negative, that we do not directly perceive 'institutions' or 'rules' – these are imposed upon us, taught to us or gradually become clear to us as patterns of behaviour, specific structurings of related concepts. The cluster of concepts I will suggest do not constitute the skeleton of a curriculum, unless for some advanced level indeed, but rather something for the teacher to have in mind and to elaborate and explicate when occasion arises. The teacher will be better able to help the pupil order and relate the disparate problems and issues of the real political world if he or she has some sketch map, at least, of basic concepts. Most of the concepts I will specify do in fact occur frequently in ordinary people's talk about politics, whether or not the same words are used. Concepts can be translated into many different language codes and conventions; but I do not believe that any would be genuinely political (meaningful in any way, for that matter), if they were not translatable. We do not need to go beyond the language of everyday life to understand and to participate in the politics of everyday life and all those things that affect it.

So to increase political literacy we need to work through everyday speech, sometimes tightening and sharpening it, sometimes unpacking its ambiguities. Political science as a discipline that aims at generalization and explanation may, indeed, need a different and a more technical vocabulary. But for this reason it has no direct relevance to increasing the political literacy of the ordinary schoolchild; and indeed I have some personal doubts if it has much to offer as a discipline in either teacher education or sixth-form work. I am surprised to find sociologists trying to teach systematic sociology in schools, rather than – perhaps – using their skills for more relevant purposes. Political scientists should not follow suit, but consider the different game of political literacy.

My suggested concepts, or rather my explanations of them, are drawn from the tradition of political philosophy far more than from political science or political sociology. Philosophers in talking about politics have usually used the ordinary language of actors in political events. (I am impressed that, for instance, John Rawls's recent account in his seminal book *Justice* (Rawls, 1972) of justice as 'fairness' very much confirms or parallels how children of about 8 or 11 talk – about football, of course: not 'what's the rule?', i.e. law, but 'is it fair?', i.e. justice. (Indeed, they can have a valid concept of 'fairness' without ever having read the rules.) Political philosophy, however, is technical in so far as, of course, it goes beyond definition of usage and meaning and attempts to establish criteria for the truth of judgements. This is not for schools, at least in any systematic way, although perhaps it should be for teacher training. 'Political literacy' merely implies using concepts clearly and sensibly and recognizing how others use them. It does *not* imply solving the problems, getting them right; it only implies understanding them and trying to have some effect. So a conceptual approach to political education does not imply knowing or doing any political philosophy. It is simply a specialized vocabulary within 'the use of English' or 'communication skills' – which is, however, the beginning of reflection, only the very beginning but the necessary beginning. So not to set the sights too high: to improve the usage and meaning of concepts, not to judge the truth of propositions or assertions using them, should be our goal; and perhaps with the most able we can consider the validity of forms of political and moral argument but hardly their truth.

There is no reason why at an advanced level these concepts cannot be treated explicitly, perhaps as the basis for a syllabus. But I cannot stress too strongly that I am not suggesting to teachers of the majority and school-leavers of earlier age groups, that they should teach these concepts explicitly or in any particular order. That is beyond my competence, and I doubt if it is desirable or possible in any systematic way. It lies in the nature of politics that there can be more plausible and sensible variations in approach than to almost any other topic (and possibly more unsensible ones too). Belief that a single method is best, or that a single usage of a concept is correct, would come close to an imposed tyranny. All we can hope for is that a relatively greater conceptual awareness, clarity and consistency will improve teaching at every level; that the ability to conceptualize and distinguish concepts is a real persuasive, moral and political skill; and that concepts can be drawn from everyday speech.

A final and important reservation: the paper only suggests concepts which are genuinely *basic* or *primary*, that is only those from which others can be derived and on which theories, generalizations, explanations and moral judgements can be based; but they are not necessarily the most important or the most widely used politically. This reservation is important and must be understood. For example, 'democracy' is plainly one of the most important concepts used in political vocabulary. But it is clearly a compound of more basic concepts – such as liberty, welfare and representation, sometimes 'rights'; even 'justice' is built into the definition. 'Equality', on the one hand, and 'tradition' or 'custom', on the other, are similar compounds. Plainly it is not much use asking, 'what is the definition of democracy or of equality, etc?', for straightaway one is faced with several different and plausible theories and doctrines about what should be done or how things should be done. It is very important to ask such questions but they can only be discussed rationally, that is, with some agreement about meaning of terms and procedures of argument, if there is some prior general agreement about what the component basic concepts mean. Hence first things first. A politically literate person must be clear what he or she means by 'democracy' or 'equality', but in order to do so political education must provide a basic vocabulary. Perhaps with advanced level pupils it is possible to begin with complex, compound concepts like 'democracy' and to 'unpack them', to work backwards to their component basic elements; but with earlier ages and abilities it is surely better to begin at the beginning.

The concepts in general

Surely the simplest perception of politics is that it is about the relationship of rulers to ruled, the few to the many, 'them and us', government and its subjects or the state and its citizens. We may wish it not to be so, but it is so. It is about differential use of and access to power over others. We start from the fact of government. But government is not a madman sitting on a sandcastle giving commands to the waves; it is men and women commanding, controlling or persuading other men and women. Whether government is prior to consent (either in time or logic), or consent prior to government is perhaps a chicken and egg problem. We want to know why such a question is asked before we try to answer it. What is clear is that all leaders need to be followed but equally clear that all large associations of people need and produce leaders. Societies without government may be a speculative possibility, but not the subject matter of ordinary politics. (One may say that the object of all politics should be the happiness of individuals. But accounts of 'politics' which begin with attempts to establish what are individual rights and how to get them tend to be notoriously unrealistic – the old civil liberties approach, which nowadays can be the potentially highly parochial 'community politics' approach.)

So we must start simultaneously with perceptions of what is done to us by government and external forces; and with perceptions of our human identity as people, what we think we are, what is due to us and what should not be done to us. And then we consider perceptions of all the different kinds of relationships there can be between rulers and ruled. Thus the very simplest and most fruitful model is found in Figure 5.1. And right from the beginning the relationship must be seen as one of mutual dependence. Leaders must have some reasonably settled organization for their welfare and protection. The more a government seeks to do, the more agents and supports it needs (particularly to wage war or to industrialize); the more people seek to do collectively even for their own good and protection, the more instruments of government they create.

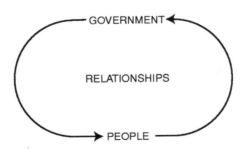

Figure 5.1

I suggest that a more elaborate model, setting out basic concepts associated with these very generalized perceptions, could be of this kind (see Figure 5.2). If this appears ridiculously

GOVERNMENT			
Power	Force	Authority	Order
RELATIONSHIPS			
Law	Justice	Representation	Pressure
PEOPLE			
Natural rights	Individuality	Freedom	Welfare

Figure 5.2

simple, (i) there are some advantages in simplicity, (ii) not so when one begins to explicate different usages of these same terms and show, for instance (as the political literacy diagram in the previous chapter suggests), how different social groups or political doctrines interpret them differently. But I do claim that an understanding of the usage and *working* of these concepts in politics could take one far and that other, more elaborate, concepts can easily be derived from them. And, once again, let us walk before we try to fly. We should try to fly, but we must learn to walk first.

Two examples: what earthly relevance has this model to those who would say either that 'politics is all a matter of class structure' or that 'politics is all a matter of tradition'? Simply this, that 'class' is, anyway, a very complex and elaborate sociological concept. Its political relevance is as a perception of a form of *order* (there are other perceived forms), and it can also be seen as a form of *representation*, the main kind of *influence* and even in extreme cases as the definition or negation of *individuality*. It is a very complex concept indeed, not as simple as it seems. We could not understand it without using more primary concepts, let alone evaluate its truth as a theory seeking to explain political behaviour. If taught first (i.e. 'before you can understand anything at all, comrade kids,

81

you must understand the concept of "class" "), it is simply imposed knowledge, the very kind of structured socialization that radical teachers object to most. Similarly 'tradition' can be seen as a particular type of claim to *authority* (the experienced should/do rule), and as a form of *representation* (history and our wise ancestors), even as a form of *welfare* (the well-being of a community is to be judged in terms of its historical continuity rather than the precise wealth or poverty of its members at any given time – otherwise, why shouldn't we sell out to the highest bidder?). It is a theory to be considered at a later stage, not a basic concept.

Let us now look at each of the terms in turn and some of their conceptual neighbours. What I cannot do is to suggest in detail what kinds of materials and what ability levels or what situations are best for illustrating which of these concepts. This can only be done by curriculum development groups of actual teachers at the various levels and by monitoring actual teaching. These 'definitions' are meant only to be useful, to furnish a starting point. 'Beware of definitions' sayeth truly Sir Karl Popper. Definitions are only proposals for usage or abbreviated accounts of usage. They cannot establish 'truth'. But I have tried to sum up a great deal of debate and to provide 'working definitions' for teacher and learner (and particularly learner–teacher) which are close to the centre of the clusters of meaning often revolving around these words; I am not deterred by the fact that many of my colleagues would come up with something different. It is about time that some- one had a go, came off the high horse and said, 'From the tradition of political philosophy and public debate about politics, in my opinion these concepts are indispensable and have these basic cores of meaning.'

The concepts specified: (i) the governing concepts

Power is, in the strongest sense, the ability to achieve a premeditated intention. Thus to have power over people is to be able to affect them in definite and defined ways. Hannah

Arendt said that all political power is, in however narrow a sense, collective, needs to carry other people with it, whether by *force* or by false or true *authority* (of which persuasion is only one form). Even a Nero or Caligula needs to keep the Palace Guard sweet and even a Nordic hero had to trust somebody while he slept. Bertrand Russell suggests that this strong sense of power as 'achieving an expressed intention' is often confused with a weak sense, that of (mere) 'unchallenge-ability'. It may be, for instance, that no one else can do it if the Prime Minister does not, but he may not be able to, for example, prevent inflation. 'Power' as unchallengeability is often mistaken for 'power' in the broader sense. If more power is accumulated in fewer hands, it does not necessarily follow that intentions can be fulfilled. Armies may fight better and workers work harder, for instance, if power is devolved. Sometimes so, sometimes not. Power can be used for good or for ill, there can be too much or too little at any given time for our own good; but a society with no concept of or use of power is inconceivable. And sometimes 'power' requires '*force*', but sometimes the force is unusable or irrelevant.

Force or coercion is when either physical pressure or weapons are actually used or when threat creates fear of use. Probably all government requires some capacity for or poten-tiality of 'force' or violence (a near synonym); but probably no government can maintain itself through time, as distinct from defence and attack at specific moments, without legitimating itself in some way, getting itself loved, respected; even just accepted as inevitable, otherwise it would need constant recourse to open violence – which is rarely the case. Again Arendt interestingly suggests that violence is at its maximum not in the concentration of political power but in its break-down. When government breaks down, violence can thrive. Now 'force', as such, is a neutral thing; it is an instrument which is used for clear or unclear purposes, for good or evil purposes. A few evil men (Fascists or types of anarchists) have made a cult of violence but it is foolish or hypocritical to think that all violence is bad. The minority pacifist argument is to be

83

considered and respected but a majority of people would agree that self-defence is justifiable, as is the use of violence in apprehending and containing criminals or in preventing greater violence. All power is not violence; all violence is not unjustifiable; and it is probably dangerous to believe that 'all power corrupts': such a nervous view goes oddly with those who want, for instance, more participation, i.e. more popular power. Max Weber did not define 'the State' (i.e. the modern state) as the monopolist of violence but as the monopolist of the 'legitimate means of violence' (which some call force). He argued that the modern state at least ensures law and order by trying to abolish private means of violence. Besides, as Milton remarked:

> Who overcomes by force
> Has overcome but half his foe.

Authority is the respect and obedience given to someone in respect of fulfilling a function which is felt to be needed and in which he or she is agreed to have excellence. If this sounds complicated it is no more than to contrast 'he knows what he's talking about' – the exercise of a function – with 'he's throwing his weight about' – the assumption of status. Thus every government seeks not merely enough *force* to defend itself but sufficient authority to legitimate itself. As Rousseau said, 'the strongest is never strong enough unless he can turn power into consent, might into obligation'. Oppressive despotisms, even, do not rule primarily by naked force but by imposing on people beliefs, typically and historically through religion and education, that they alone can fulfil functions which are thought to be necessary (e.g. they embody the commands of the gods – who may not exist; they defend the country against barbarian hordes – who may be quite unwarlike; they ensure that harvests will be gathered and corn stored and that irrigation takes place – when the peasants might anyway do these things for them; or that they alone can preserve order – when other forms of order, both better and worse, are readily possible). Authority can be legitimate or illegitimate, false or true, depending on how free people are to question the alleged needs and functions of government, to recognize alternatives and to judge how well the functions are being fulfilled. Authority – is it needful to say? – is not necessarily *authoritarian*. All authority is not bad, neither is it good *per se*; it is ordinarily thought of as legitimate authority when (i) its powers are derived from commonly accepted procedures; (ii) it does not suppress discussion of alternative ways both of defining and fulfilling needs; and (iii) it does not seek to extend its functionally defined powers generally into any or every concern. For example, the authority I have as a university teacher is because students want to study and, in varying degrees, respect my competence; but that competence does not extend to laying down the law about their morals. The functions of a primary school teacher, on the other hand, are far more general and less specific: his or her authority is much more general, and more like that of a parent. Hence the greater difficulties. The limits of proper authority are then far harder to define. Or consider Dylan Thomas's old and blind Captain Catt in *Under Milk Wood*: 'Damn you, the mulatto woman, she's mine. Who's captain here?' For the implied answer is that a different kind of functionally defined competence would be called for in a low-down bar than that which gave him the unquestioned captaincy in keeping his dirty British coaster afloat in mad March gales, etc.

Order is the most general perception that rational expectations about political, social and economic relationships, almost whatever they are, will be fulfilled. Disorder is when one does not know what is going to happen next, or more strictly when uncertainties are so numerous as to make rational premeditation or calculation appear impossible. Faced with disorder, the radical philosopher Bentham said, 'mankind will choose any kind of "order", however unjust'. 'Order' is, in this sense, a prerequisite of any kind of government at all, good or bad. *Justice*, *rights*, *welfare*, all need 'order'; and even *freedom* (as we will suggest) becomes trivial or simply ineffective if there is no reasonably settled context. But the concept is morally completely neutral. It is simply knowing where one stands, however bad and oppressive the system ('at least one knows where one stands' – which is no excuse, for the same could be true in a better system). Only a lunatic would attack *order* as such, or could possibly adjust to a complete breakdown of expectations; but those who justify 'order' as such, rather than simply point out its minimal necessity, are usually smuggling into the concept their own particular ideas of the best form that 'order' should take. And prophecies that 'all order will break down if something isn't done about it' – whatever it is – are notoriously rhetorical and alarmist. Concepts of *disorder* can best be elaborated as specific negations of 'order'. I mean that different types of disorder are best understood in terms of what they are challenging rather than as things in themselves; nor should we necessarily assume that they are instruments to some other purpose; for their main purpose may be to protest against the existing form of 'order'. I would suggest that these negations of 'order' could be seen as some kind of continuum from *public opinion, pressure, strike, boycott, parade, demo, rebellion,* coup d'état, *war of independence, civil war,* through to *revolution.* And that each of these concepts has specific and limiting characteristics; in other words, *violence* is rarely uncontrolled and explosive, it is usually intended and specific. 'Ungovernable fury' is usually fairly deliberate. Ideas of how much types of violence threaten 'order' are highly conventional and historically specific. Some people today fear 'a breakdown of law and order' from a degree of violence on the streets which was easily tolerable (if disliked) in the eighteenth century. And in some of the Arab kingdoms of the early Muslim era, civil war and fratricide were the recognized institutions for settling the succession to the throne.

The concepts specified: (ii) the popular concepts

(So far looking, as it were, down from government; but now

looking up from the people. Basically we want government both to do things for us and to keep its distance.)

Natural rights (or basic rights) are what we claim as the minimum conditions for a proper human existence. 'Life, liberty and property', said John Locke, or 'life, liberty and the pursuit of happiness', said Thomas Jefferson. Thomas Hobbes was even more minimal: man only had two rights, which were absolute – 'by all means to defend himself' and 'to seek peace and preserve it', in other words life itself, our basic human individuality, is all we have by natural right. As with *order*, there is a great temptation to stuff into the concept everything one desires – the 'right to an eight-hour day and a five-day week', for instance; but clarity of discourse is likely to be greater the fewer basic assumptions we make. By all means demand an eight-hour day or five-day week, but such demands should be conceived as *welfare*, one possible thing that we wish for among others beyond our basic or natural rights.

Many of the things we call 'our rights' are, more correctly, seen as things the law allows us to enjoy (like free speech) or commands others to provide for us (like education); such legal rights are beyond number. And political rights are simply the minimum conditions needed for citizens (as defined by legal rights) to be politically effective – so these will vary vastly, depending on who are citizens and what the role of citizenship is thought to be. The Greeks of the fifth century BC valued political rights so much that they actually said that a man not fit to exercise them was not really, or properly a man – but a natural slave. But 'a man's a man for a' that', as Robert Burns (following Rousseau) sees better than Aristotle. The basic concept must refer to what we think all legal and political systems should allow, indeed enhance; and to what are our rights simply as individual human beings. But, of course, man is a sociable animal, so some would argue that perhaps groups can have 'natural rights'. Religions, ethnic groups and nations are the most usual claimants. Opinions differ greatly but I am sceptical of this; their legal rights can be or should be justified on other grounds. Their precise formulation, and hence application, is historically specific rather than universal (if they are natural 'rights' then is there a right not to have a religion or not to be a member of a nation, or to change either?). The family is sometimes considered by some to have rights that are prior to those of its individual members (but this may be confusing biological and cultural need with moral judgements – I cannot avoid having been in a family and obviously should have some special obligation to it; but haven't I also on certain conditions a right to break from it?). What is worrying about the idea that groups have natural rights, rather than negotiated legal rights, is that it implies rights against individual members, usually women.

Individuality as a concept is closely related to the concept of natural rights but it is what we perceive as unique to each man and possibly to mankind. The content of the concept varies greatly from society to society. Ours is 'individualistic' in a sense almost unknown to the medieval or ancient world to whom in many ways group loyalties were more significant than individuality. We commonly believe that the object of our political activity is the happiness of 'individuals' and sometimes we even believe that actions and opinions can be justified for no other reason than that they are authentic manifestations of individuality, sincere expressions of personality. Marxists teach that 'the individual' is an imminent category and will only be truly free and individual in the classless society when all oppression ends; and liberals preach that actual individual self-interest is the only possible measure, in the here and now, of the goodness of public policies.

Conservatives tend to be more sceptical about 'man as the measure of all things' and to share with some Socialists a sense that community is more important than individualism. But individualism ('thou shalt be as individual as thou can be') or the cult of 'personality' may simply be a caricature or unnecessary extension of individuality. It is hard to conceive of a community that was not composed of, in some sense, biological units exhibiting 'individuality'; but they will not necessarily believe in individualism.

'Individuality' is one of the most difficult concepts to get across in our present society, because an often militant, self-centred individualism is so much assumed to be natural. We should respect individual differences while being fully aware how much we tend to exaggerate them. (I find that to discuss 'the attempt to dress differently' is a good way to sharpen this perception: the paradox that it all ends up so much alike and that the new clothes do not ensure new or radically different personalities.) No species in nature differs less in physical attributes from member to member than man, yet can differ more in character or psychology. [We all have a common humanity, but we are all unique.]

Freedom in its weaker or negative sense is being free from arbitrary or unwanted control or intervention but in its stronger or more positive sense it is actually making choices and doing things in a self-willed and uncoerced way. Modern liberalism has tended to stress 'freedom from', as if being left alone as an individual is the best thing to hope for. But the classical idea of 'freedom' was tied to the concept of citizenship, indeed to political activity itself; a free man was someone who takes part in public life in an uncoerced way. Far from 'freedom' being 'the recognition of necessity', things that we must do can hardly be called free actions. 'Necessity, the tyrant's plea', said Milton. Some 'freedom' in a negative sense may exist in autocracies, between the gaps of the law as the indifference of the ruler or the inefficiency or corruption of the bureaucracy. While in totalitarian societies 'freedom' is actually denounced as an illusion (or else praised to the skies as a great far future event), everything in theory is held to be determined by economic or racial factors. But genuine 'freedom' depends on some distinction and interplay between private and public life. We have to believe that some things (though they will vary from society to society) are private, not of public concern, and that people are free to immerse themselves in private life; but 'freedom' is obviously endangered if most or many do not choose to participate in public life. In free societies participation is voluntary for each

89

individual, but it is – in greatly varying degrees – encouraged; and it is functionally necessary for such societies that freedom has to be practised, not just enjoyed, that we have a duty as human beings to make use of our right. When this actually occurs, of course, it can be disturbing for all who govern, manage or teach.

Welfare is the belief that the prosperity and happiness of communities and individuals beyond mere physical survival should be the concern of governments. The concept of *needs* is much the same perception and like *rights* both seem to express something which if minimal is almost self-evident, but when elaborated and detailed become infinitely arguable – all the desirable things that the state *could* do for us, at a cost (both of resources and liberty). The 'common good' (which Aquinas stipulated as an object of human government) is close to 'welfare' and as seemingly necessary but as specifically ambiguous. The provision of 'bread' (or whatever is the staple food) is almost universally agreed to be a legitimate demand by individuals upon governments. 'Health' is a very recent candidate – disease and pestilence were once seen as uncontrollable, certainly by governments, perhaps not by prayer or sacrifice. 'Employment' is very modern – only in the 1930s did people begin to believe that periodic cycles or spasms of unemployment were avoidable at all, and some are still not convinced. Education and minimal care of children are now hard to avoid; they are firmly seen, both by governments and governed, as parts of 'welfare'.

Everyone wants more 'welfare'. It seems a self-evident good. But there are two entailments of the concept which cause difficulties: (i) Whereas some 'rights' may be basic to all humanity, 'welfare' is always a package with differing contents. What goes into the package must be considered both economically and morally in terms of a price to be paid in terms of other concepts, values and goods: we live in a world of finite resources and potentially infinite demand. (ii) It is possible for governments to smother people in 'welfare' in order to keep them quiet and politically passive. A century and a half ago Alexis de Tocqueville imagined that despotisms in the future would not exploit their subjects so much as seek to satiate them or keep them full of well-being and entertainment, to do almost anything for them, except to let them govern themselves or enjoy *freedom*. ('Bread *and* circuses', as it were. Some see 'the consumer society' in this way.) Ernest Gellner has recently called our society a 'Danegeld State', and has earlier argued that the legitimacy of all governments in the modern world almost entirely depends upon their ability to increase the standard of living ('The social contract in search of an idiom: The demise of the Danegeld State', *Political Quarterly*, April–June 1975). Of course 'welfare' and 'rights' must progress and go hand in hand; but as concepts they are distinct from 'individuality' and 'freedom' with which they must always be balanced, compromised, related, synthesized – use whatever word you think is best.

The concepts specified: (iii) the relating concepts

(Each of these concepts covers a wide range of institutions and beliefs that relate governed to government, and each of them looks different when viewed from on top or from below.)

Law is the body of general rules, commands, prohibitions and entitlements made by or recognized by government, published and enforced by it and recognized as binding (even if not as *just*) by those whom they can apply to. This definition is complex, largely because I do not believe that people ordinarily regard 'law' simply as the particular command or will of a sovereign – this is a pseudo-realism ('law' must be general, published and recognized as binding, i.e. not 'Off with his head' but 'Be it enacted that all those playing croquet who hit the ball of the Queen of Hearts, whether by chance, accident, design or deliberate intent, either of themselves or of others, whether people or beasts, shall forthwith be beheaded, if it so pleaseth Her Majesty'). Yet the famous 'positive theory of law', that law is the command of the sovereign, is at least half-right; if people do not ordinarily confuse 'law' with mere command, yet they do not confuse it with 'justice' either. Laws can be seen as valid and yet unjust. 'Off with his head' is not law at all; but the 'Be it enacted . . .' as above is clearly a 'law', even if an unjust one.

'Constitutional law' is a very complex concept, neither a basic concept nor an especially suitable beginning for an understanding of politics. And 'the Rule of Law' is either a truism, that there should be laws (but about what?) or else is a politically very tendentious assertion that we should ordinarily obey a law simply because it is the 'law'. Others would argue that we should always consider whether or not laws are just before we obey them. Somehow both the positions seem extreme in practice.

Many people say that any civilized behaviour necessarily presupposes belief in 'a rule of law', that is obedience to rules – so that even if the rules are unjust, we should only try to change them according to accepted rules. (Sometimes this is the *only* concept introduced into political education when taught – so incompletely – as 'British Constitution' or 'The Institutions of the British Government'.) But two problems arise: (i) What if the rules are so constituted as to avoid change or to make it deliberately difficult? (ii) Is it true that all complex activities presuppose legal rules? Consider again 'fairness' and the young footballer: he learns to play football by playing football, not by reading the rules (try learning to play croquet by learning the rules!) and his concept of what is fair (or just) does not in fact depend on knowing all the rules (only on observing behaviour and convention), nor logically need it – for the rules could be unjust, ambiguous or self-contradictory. Anyway, the 'rule of law', like 'democracy' (the one usually conservative, the other usually radical), is arguably anything but a primary or a basic concept.

Justice or what is right is the most important and complex of concepts into which everyone intrudes their own values; but generally speaking what is just is what people accept as done fairly even if they are either ignorant of the outcome of the process or are even personally disadvantaged. 'Is this a fair way to decide?' usually means the same as 'Is this a just way to decide?' Analogies and comparisons are more often invoked than absolute standards or first principles. To deal with people justly or fairly is always to deal with them consistently relative to other cases and to changed circumstances. When absolute standards or first principles are invoked, they have to be applied to concrete problems; so inevitably the application will involve comparisons, relativities, calculations of the probable consequences, and – most important morally – consideration of other people's standards and principles. How easy it would be if 'idealism' were always confronted with 'naked self-interest' which anyway usually wears fig leaves of many colours. 'To temper justice with mercy' is usually to confuse *law* with 'justice'. For 'law', as general rules, needs mercy, forgiveness or justifiable exceptions to be morally acceptable; but the concept of 'justice' ordinarily includes all these already. All political doctrines are concerned with social justice, or the proper distribution of goods, rewards and punishments of all kinds. Political doctrines are necessarily accounts both of what can or could be the case and of what should be the case. Hence nearly every relationship possible between ruler and ruled is perceived in some way as concerned with 'justice'.

Representation is the most general justification for why a few may rule many or for how the many try to control the few in terms of embodying some external attribute. But there are many more external attributes validating claims to represent than to represent 'the people'. Historically most governments claimed to represent the will of the gods or of God. Others have claimed authority because they are representative of a race or caste, a tribe or a family, a class or a nation; or of reason or of either inherited or acquired skills; or of traditional areas, of property, interests, the 'general will', the Party, 'the People' or of individuals. And all of the claims can be put in the form that representation is either a mandated delegation, or else a responsible discretion. The matter is complicated but not infinitely so. If people have claimed that their *power* is representative for other reasons, then I have missed them. My point is simply that the concept is of far wider applicability than 'representative institutions' in parliamentary or electoral senses. A 'representative of people' should also beware that he may be representing government to the people quite as much as he represents the people to the government. 'Representative institutions', indeed, can both control and actually strengthen governments. It is a two-way business. 'Representation' is not just to be seen then as a right of the people, it can also be a necessity of power. 'Because we wish to build the Federal pyramid to a great height', said one of the participants in the Philadelphia Convention, 'its roots must go deep.'

Pressure constitutes all those means by which government and people can influence each other politically for specified purposes, other than force or law directly. Force or law may both be used as threats: if expressed public opinion, persuasion, example, economic, social or psychological influence fail or falter, then 'force' may 'have to' follow or the 'law' will 'have to' be changed. But public opinion, persuasion, example, economic, social and psychological influence are the normal forms of 'pressure'. To exert 'pressure', organization is ordinarily called for, thus parties and pressure groups are the most important institutionalized forms of 'pressure'. But to stress institutions exclusively, as often happens in introductory teaching, is to make the same kind of mistake as when *representation* is remorselessly narrowed to electoral systems from the word go: both comprehension and imagination are limited. Certainly there is an element of unreality in assuming any longer that most political pressures in our society come from the parties, even perhaps from the obvious pressure groups. And pressure is not merely exercised through representative institutions, it is exercised through the Press and the other media, indeed, books still count surprisingly: and it is exercised privately just by words and gestures. Types of disorder (see 'order', page 85 above) are also, when used as threats for limited and defined ends, types of 'pressure'. And

Table 5.1 Summary of basic concepts

Government:

Power
The ability to achieve an intended effect either by force or more usually by claims to authority.

Force
Physical pressure or use of weapons to achieve an intended effect – latent in all government, constant in none.

Authority
Respect and obedience given by virtue of an institution, group or person fulfilling a function agreed to be needed and which he or it has superior knowledge or skill.

Order
When expectations are fulfilled and calculations can be made without fear of all the circumstances and assumptions changing.

Relationships:

Law
The body of general rules made, published and enforced by governments and recognized as binding by the government even if not as just.

Justice
What is due to people as the result of some process accepted as fair irrespective of the outcome.

Representation
The claim for the few to represent the many because they embody some external attribute, of which popular consent is only one of many.

Pressure
All the means by which government and people influence each other, other than by law or by force.

People:

Natural rights
The minimum conditions for proper human existence – prior even to legal and political rights.

Individuality
What we perceive as unique to each man and mankind – to be distinguished from individualism, a purely nineteenth-century doctrine.

Freedom
The making of choices and doing things of public significance in a self-willed and uncoerced way.

Welfare
The belief that the prosperity and happiness of individuals and communities is a concern of government, not merely survival.

there is not merely the stick but also the carrot; praise is a form of pressure as great as blame, criticism or threat. Almost any kind of 'pressure', like 'force', can be justified *in some circumstances*, provided that the object of the pressure is definable, specific and potentially reliable.

What is all that about?

Two words of warning. To understand concepts is not to understand society, but only a preliminary step. To understand a society and its political system is to understand the *working* of its dominant concepts and their relationships.

To say again, I do not advocate the direct teaching or learning of concepts except perhaps at an advanced level (anyway, definitions of concepts can be learned by rote as easily as constitutional rules and conventions). All I advocate is a far greater conceptual awareness in interpreting material in any study of politics from the simplest component of early school right up to A levels. Curriculum development should build in issues, cases and problems that establish and sharpen some such concepts and distinctions as I have tried to make. A large part of political literacy will consist in exposing the presuppositions of assertions about institutions and needs which claim to be purely factual and descriptive (but having exposed them, of course, it does not follow that all repressions are bad, as Marcuse once sweepingly assumed: some would do better for themselves if exposed to critical light, some not).

A further paper will argue that there are five concepts which must be treated as 'procedural values', that is as preconditions of political literacy or necessary assumptions of any political education which is not simply indoctrination or imposed socialization. [See Chapter 10.]

6 Citizenship and education

This is a slightly expanded version of an address given in 1992 to the twenty-fifth annual conference of the Politics Association of which I was the first President. The kick in the tail at this worthy body for becoming overly engaged in sixth-form examination teaching shows me moving from the narrow concept of 'Politics' teaching of the earlier essays, still somewhat disciplinary, and putting 'political literacy' into a broader concept of teaching for citizenship.

My concern is not with the kind of citizenship that is appropriate to an autocracy, nor with how the idea of free citizenship can sustain itself under autocracy – as the events of 1989 in Eastern Europe so dramatically demonstrated, against the expectations of all expert opinion: that in itself is a vindication of freedom. I am concerned with true citizenship, the idea of individuals interacting for public purposes in a civic community: the citizenship associated with the existence and exercise of civil liberties by free people.

Historically there have been two main ideas of civil liberties and of the kind of citizenship appropriate to each of them: the one, sometimes called 'liberal', that civil liberties are a framework of law to protect individuals against the state; and the other, sometimes called republican, that civil liberties are the positive means by which citizens may influence affairs of state. Much educational practice still falls under the first paradigm, despite a remarkable revival of scholarly interest in the republican tradition (Pocock, 1975; Heater, 1990; Oldfield, 1990; Skinner, 1998). In the last two years of the reign of Margaret Thatcher, the concept of citizenship stepped onto the political agenda of Britain in an unexpected manner. Government ministers suddenly began urging a distinctive idea of active citizenship. Foreign observers might be pardoned any surprise that a debate on the nature of citizenship is, for the majority of people in British public life, such a late, sudden and enigmatic guest at the feast. But then Britain is not the United States nor France neither, two countries whose very national identity is still perceived in the light of different ideas, or myths if you prefer, of active citizenship – originally indeed a revolutionary tradition, bourgeois revolutions, but like those of 1989, revolutions none the less. To them even the mild word 'active' in 'active citizenship' should be quite unnecessary. What else is a citizen, would say John Doe or Jean François, than someone who is active in public affairs? Indeed, but let us not exaggerate: modern American and French citizens are not a hyperactive ancient Athenian citizen elite; yet they know that there is a kind of official, even constitutional, blessing on being at least spasmodically active; or at least not feeling peculiar if they are.

In Britain, however, the qualifying adjective for citizen has less often been 'active' than 'good'. Good citizens have a respect for law and order, pay their taxes (even poll taxes) know their place in society (what the philosopher F. H. Bradley called, in a once-celebrated essay, 'My station and its duties'), keep their noses clean and are ever so grateful to be governed so well; although we British do rather pride ourselves (or used to) on knowing our rights. And these rights are held to include civil liberties, but then liberties perceived as part of a legal order, not primarily a political or a citizen order. We should be able to go to court to protect ourselves not merely from nuisances by strangers or neighbours or public bodies, but even against the state. Only recently on environmental issues have neighbours begun to combine for political or 'community' action.

There can be, of course, a good Conservative case for a constitution to protect our rights against radical innovations, just as there is now – and quite a novelty – a radical or republican case to reform the constitution in order to enable a positive and participative citizenship. I refer, of course, to Lord Hailsham's former views on Parliament as an 'elected despotism' and to the Charter 88 movement. The House of Lords has just opined that it would be a good idea to set down our rights in fundamental law just to be sure what they are, and Charter 88 adds that we might as well improve them a bit while we are trying to find them in order to embalm them. But too many good Brits believe that if our rights are well protected by the courts and not heavily abused by the state, as on the whole they think they are not, we can stay safely in our homes, even in our Welsh or Highland second homes, and sing madrigals, watch the television, make love, even walk the streets safely at night (so long as you are not a woman), or otherwise kill the time pleasantly without public obligations.

Less than a century ago the matter was clearer because editorials would habitually refer, on the one hand, to the restive and excessively democratic American or French republican spirit (which everyone knew did not simply mean no monarch; indeed, a republican spirit famously existed in Holland and other lands where there was a monarch); and on the other hand, leader writers before the First World War would flatter their British readers as 'good subjects' or 'loyal subjects'. I believe it was the slaughter and the conscription crisis in 1916 that turned official rhetoric from 'subjects of the King' to, well, not quite 'fellow citizens' but at least citizens of the realm, 'British citizens'. But nowadays, even when Mrs Thatcher used to talk with admirable realism if gross constitutional impropriety about 'my ministers', she would never say ' my subjects'; indeed, incredibly she spasmodically began to demand that people should exhibit more citizenship. Citizenship was held up as an individual moral virtue. Suddenly the idea of 'the good citizen', which hitherto was simply that of being 'the good subject' who voted occasionally in

99

public elections, has proved insufficient even for a Conservative view of things. Douglas Hurd, Kenneth Baker and Chris Patten stretched their minds to elaborate this primal thought of citizenship as an individual moral virtue in speeches which are at least wonderfully useful as essay assignments by political philosophers to average students.

By citizenship Mrs Thatcher meant that individuals have a duty to help strangers as well as family, especially those less well off. Rights and duties are morally correlative, and so they should be; each implies the other, both John Stuart Mill and Emmanuel Kant said that; so far so good. But they should be done by individuals voluntarily, and when so done they enhance the individual. In Hurd's version, that was the main object; but Chris Patten's variant had a hint or a hope that it actually helps others. All agreed, however, that voluntarism is the mark of moral citizenship. Helping others must not be done, or as little as possible, by public authorities out of all our pockets, nor by churches from moral blackmail based on eccentric – so they say – and unministerial readings of the Scriptures.

Now as often with Margaret Thatcher – her critics still ignore this at their peril – there was a thumping big half-truth here. Let us say a reverential 'Amen' to a half-truth and let those of us who are without sin cast the first civil-disobedient stone. Why has the Labour Party (which, for better or for worse, in sickness and health, is my own party) not made a virtue of active, republican citizenship; or not until very, very recently, and then in a tentative and intellectually unimpressive manner? Presumably because it has long been possessed by a crusading spirit to get hold of the centres of power to use them in the interests of the poor, the dispossessed, the disadvantaged and the handicapped (or should I now say 'to manage a mixed economy more efficiently'?). If standards of secondary education had not fallen (as is now matter of faith to all British statesmen) I could have put that more briefly in Latin by saying that they too share the *libido dominandi*. But this crusading spirit, while a generous impulse in practice, often meant a cocksure knowingness about what was best for other people. 'We know what people want because we have been elected; how else could we have been elected?', say the old councillors. Or as the poet Auden once put it, 'we are all here on earth to help each other, but what the others are here for, God only knows.' The old Labour project also carried with it a formidable commitment to using, indeed strengthening, central power – as shown by the divisions of the Scottish Labour Party in 1978 and 1979, and a continued ambivalence about any radical devolution or Home Rule.

For the Thatcherite half-truth is that people are very open to the suggestion that they would rather, if empowered, help themselves than be helped and to choose for themselves when to help others and whom. The idea of a public-welfare society as a gift of the state did begin to grate; or could be seen, even by some of its managers and clients, either to be overdone or to be so full of accumulated historical accidents and anomalies (like the supplementary benefit regulations) as to have lost all coherence, hence comprehensibility, hence self-confident or self-evident justification.

The half-untruth in Thatcher's rhetoric of citizenship is, however, the belief that voluntary effort can fill the gap left by the deliberate underresourcing of social services, especially those associated with local authorities as a plurality of centres of power, and those where the 'clients' are the least able to organize themselves in effective pressure groups: the very old, the very young, the mentally and physically handicapped and the long-term unemployed. So suddenly the ancient idea of positive citizenship becomes confused with charity, or is seen as part of privatization; and privatization not just of industry but of large parts of the social services, public responsibility for the arts, industrial training, health and education. The remaining public-welfare bodies are asked to work with voluntary bodies, as in the Griffith Report on caring for the elderly. And being so underresourced, they have little choice, however spasmodic, insufficient, sentimental, eccentric or commercially self-interested the voluntary support can prove to be.

None the less, there has always been a good involvement of volunteers in areas of need. It would be hard to envisage any state of affairs where extra volunteers cannot help (even in schools); at the very least, sit with and talk to the lonely, or shop for those infirm and foolish enough not to have loving families, tasks well within the capabilities even of untrained people of common sense and common feeling. It is good to help others and it gives us a feeling for others. Professionalism in the social services has sometimes discredited itself. The real needs of clients can be confounded by a claim to professionalism that is a mixture of old battles for disciplinary status and relatively new (for the professions) trade union concerns. This is another question. But undoubtedly the public is sometimes confused as to whether they are being harangued to save the NHS or to save NUPE. This has given the new perverse sense of citizenship its opportunity and plausibility.

The new sense of citizenship as individual voluntary social or charitable work is perverse for one obvious reason, and one less obvious but more profound that goes to the heart of the dilemmas of our culture. The obvious reason is that in a mainly voluntary system in no way can resources be matched to needs or rational priorities followed – indeed logically it could not be a 'system' at all. Priorities would, figuratively speaking, follow whether the Princess Anne or Glenda Jackson broadcasts 'The Week's Good Cause' rather than how good it is. Certainly each of us have a moral and civic duty to give (as 'giving' is extolled as a virtue in placards in American buses and subways), whether from the private pocket, the corporate cheque book or the widow's mite. All that is easy, but to engage ourselves, with hands, feet and head as well as purse and heart, to commit precious time and physical effort to regular voluntary work, this would be, on the scale needed, highly demanding to ordinary individuals and could also be highly threatening to the conventional state.

It could threaten because if people did engage their own time and effort, then they would surely do so, be they ever so law-abiding good subjects, *critically*. They may come to think about what they are doing, not just do it as in a routinized job. The heart and the head, not just the purse, would want a say both in *what* should be done and in *how* it should be done. And this points to the deeper inadequacy and incoherence of the new view. For if the voluntary involvement of masses of people under the banner of 'citizenship' in the running of the social services is crucial and critical, people will become critically minded and will expect to find some effective forum in which to air their criticism; or, still worse, if part of the criticism is that there is no such forum, or only a quite ineffective one, then they may want to make one. And the volunteers themselves, nominated in the twin names of indivi- dualism and economy, may themselves become effective lob- byists for more public resources. Deciding how the edict on spelling is going to be implemented will not mend the school roof. In other words, no idea of citizenship can be totally individualized, removed from a public realm, removed from a common-sense sense that some things can only be done publicly; and, further, then to have any public effect means (in Hannah Arendt's simple argument) 'acting in concert' (Arendt, 1970). What on earth is he talking about? Come down to earth! Well, she started it: 'there is no such thing as society', said the former Prime Minister.

Citizenship cannot be re-presented as charitable work. Giving by individuals is in itself a good thing and it can make us each feel more virtuous or less guilty, which is no bad thing: but it is only when individuals combine through active citizen- ship that both public policy and private behaviour can be influenced. Free societies must debate, and a constantly shift- ing debate it is: what is the proper sphere of the private and the public, the individual and the social; or in economic terms, what is the most efficient and the most acceptable mix of a mixed economy? Public decisions have too important an effect on the lives of individuals to be left entirely to a multiplication of random individual decisions with the government pretend- ing to be the mere umpire of natural market forces.

Public decisions are too important to be left to governments

103

alone, especially to governments that try to narrow to the absolute minimum the extent of these benefits, goods and services that can only be provided, or most efficiently provided, publicly; and while mocking 'society' a 'community' is invoked into whom the long-term mentally ill can be discharged. While the concept of society should not, indeed (the half-truth again), be used as an excuse for avoiding individual responsibility ('I'm not to blame, it was society; it was me upbringing', etc.), surely a sense of sociability in individuals is a virtue as well as a psycho-biological human characteristic; or to use an old-fashioned political and military word, 'fraternity'. The radical Right will allow one legitimate area of non-individualistic, non-competitive, altruistic behaviour: the family. That is one reason why they make so much of it. But, remarkably, some parents try to bring their children up to care for others; and families by themselves can as easily be hunting packs of nepotism and special advantage as they can be schools of virtue.

It follows that any education for citizenship must involve both education and the training for effect on public issues through acting together. If we educate for citizenship we may get citizens, individuals who are interactive and publicly active. Citizens' actions, like all free actions, are unpredictable; government in a citizen culture becomes less easy to conduct, but perhaps more effective and more interesting when it has to and can carry people with it. People are more interested in following and working for results, in politics as much as sport, which are not foregone conclusions. I don't think we should sound solemn and say that with more political education democracy will work better. Who knows? Some exercise of civil liberties may destabilize some governments. Tough.

By civil liberties I mean those things we need to be able to do without interference from the state in order to maintain what we ordinarily call a free society, or what J. S. Mill called 'representative government'. Note that civil liberties are more specific and many than human rights. Human rights are few and basic. No modern philosopher doubts that, but in the classroom 'rights' are multiplied, used and abused promiscuously. Yet it obscures clear thinking and takes away any sense of cost from moral choices to call everything we want, everything we think to be a need or think good, a human right. What it is to be a human being is not necessarily to be a fully paid-up or fully supported, credit-card-carrying member of consumer society; or even of a democracy. Inhabitants of autocracies have human rights, even supporters of autocracies, even enemies. Wants and basic needs are to be distinguished, just as civil rights and human rights should not be confused. Human rights are few and are universal moral imperatives; civil rights are many and specific and relative to particular societies. Advanced civil rights may set a general goal and a standard, but they are not inherent to human nature. They are historical and cultural achievements. To call everything we want or think good a right confuses understanding, and stakes a claim without delineating a means.

Let me draw a practical inference from this abstract point. I see both advocacy and the teaching of civil liberties and citizenship not as a campaign for everything we think as right, nor (as philosophers would say) for substantive values but for procedural values. A Council for Civil Liberties (now called 'Liberty') was once unwise enough to confuse matters by commenting, for instance, on the truth of Mr Duncan Campbell's allegations about the covert activities of our famous national security forces, rather than on his right to make allegations, whether true or false, and the methods by which the government tried to stop him. Nor was it wise to comment on the justice of the miners' strike, still less to allow no criticism of their tactics and behaviour, but only those of the police. As citizens we can and should comment loudly on the policies of the state, but to protect civil liberties as *educators* we must make our remarks strictly relevant, but then to make them all the more strong, to *the procedures and methods* of the state and its agents. Civil liberties enable free politics to be pursued, participative citizenship to be

105

practised and, in extreme cases, basic human rights to be defended.

All this calls, however, for the encouragement of and a training for political action, not simply 'respect for the rule of law', as is so often said. Does 'political action' sound too harsh? I don't see why. Aristotle regarded all relevant analysis, criticism and public speech as a form of action. No one has ever tried to teach action as an end in itself. No one (except some anarchists and all Dadaists) favours mindless, thought-less, unpremeditated, instinctive action. But equally, if it is citizenship we are concerned with (and not just routine teaching for 'good results' in an examination syllabus), the teacher cannot be held responsible for the use the young citizen makes of his acquired knowledge and skills, or rather the emphasis should be, skills and knowledge. Again, the actions of free men and women are unpredictable (Arendt, 1958). If we teach to induce the correct substantive attitudes (whether 'respect for the rule of law', 'proper individualism', 'the classless society' or whatever), it is not politics or citizen-ship we are teaching: it is something at best paternally approved, our quasi-autocratic friend, the 'good citizen', say rather 'good subject'. And at worst it is, indeed, attempted indoctrination. Successive government ministers instinctively disliked the educational value of empathy because it obviously implies a sympathetic understanding of alternatives. Of course, the word favoured on all sides is not 'action' but is 'participation'. I've no objection, so long as watching is not thought to be, however knowledgeable the spectator, as participative and healthy as having a share in the action. Citizenship is among a rather small group of important human actions in which anyone can have a share in the action, unless of course, as in so many happy lands, restrained by fear of force.

Unhappily, government opinion [in the 1980s] still leans towards a late Victorian view of citizenship education as being concerned primarily with good behaviour rather than active participation. The [then] Speaker of the House of Commons set up late in 1988 a Commission on Citizenship which reported in 1990. The recommendations of the Report seemed very close to the kind of ministerial thinking discussed at the beginning of this sermon. Its recommendations envisaged education for a world of voluntary service and community service, in which any political decisions are made purely by elective representatives of the people in Parliament (and 'Parliament is sovereign' whatever we've signed up to, whatever the European Court of Justice says) and any ambiguities in legislation are decided by courts and must, of course, not merely be respected but obeyed. The individual is protected by the laws. He has little need to do anything by way of corporate action: pressure groups and parties were never mentioned!

Quoting a comparative empirical survey, they said with pride:

> On responsibilities, the views of the British citizen were clear: 'Far and away the most commonly cited British duty, however, was obedience to the law ... combined with a more general emphasis on civility or obedience to community norms.
>
> (Commission on Citizenship, 1990)

Early nineteenth-century satirists had an alternative version of John Bull called Lickspittle. Happily this empirical reaffirmation of an alleged English national characteristic is at least problematic. The true behavioural test is behaviour, not simply expressed attitudes. At the time the Commission was polishing up its far too anodyne report, the Scottish poll tax rebellion was spreading to England, eventually bringing down a Prime Minister. But it is probably right; most people, if not 'the British citizen' (as an imaginative corporate entity), obey the law simply because it is the law, as if Socrates and all the political philosophers had never lived to draw a distinction between law and justice, to point out courageously that the state is not always right. But to the extent that that is true, it points to the problem Britain faces, not to the fortunate inherited solution. It is the difficult task of a genuine citizen

107

education to shake this bland belief that good citizenship consists *simply* in some voluntary service and a general respect for the rule of law. Yes, indeed. If the laws are good laws. I cannot examine all laws and how they are interpreted and enforced, so pragmatically I give them the benefit of the doubt – with that reservation. May I quote from *Political Education and Political Literacy* on this point crucial to the character of our political culture?

> Many people say that any civilized behaviour necessarily presupposes a belief in a 'rule of law', that is obedience to rules – so that even if the rules are unjust, we should only try to change them according to accepted rules. (Sometimes this is the only concept introduced into political education when taught – so incompletely – as 'British Constitution' or 'The Institutions of British Government'.) But two problems arise: (i) what if the rules are so constituted to avoid change? (ii) Is it true that all complex activities presuppose legal rules? Consider again 'fairness' and the young footballer: he learns to play football by playing football, not by reading the rules ... and his concept of what is fair (or just) does not in fact depend on knowing all the rules (only on observing behaviour and convention), nor logically need it – for the rules could be unjust, ambiguous or self-contradictory.
>
> (Crick and Porter, 1978)

The Commission on Citizenship carefully avoided any discussion as to whether the rules are just or can be changed – any incitement to thought: 'As we have said, in the UK there is no comprehensive list of entitlements. Individuals' freedoms exist to the extent that Parliament has not enacted restrictions.' How can any group of so-called citizens say that without even raising the possibility that some legitimately enacted restrictions have gone too far, or even hinting that every other country in the European Community has a ligitable human rights legislation? [As now we do.] Was this handpicked group nervous or excessively conventional? It is actually easier to think freely in most classrooms.

Even an Education Minister could be more imaginative and

state the problem better. Mr Alan Howarth, MP (then Parliamentary Under-Secretary of State for Education) addressed the Politics Association on its twenty-first anniversary:

> The issue of politics in the classroom seems to me part of a wider one of how to encourage discrimination (in the best sense of the term), good sense, and rational judgement in young people ... It is never going to be easy. It has to be faced squarely that political education entails consideration of politics and politics is about choices which so affect the lives of citizens that emotions are likely to run high.
>
> (Howarth, 1992)

'Citizenship' was mentioned as a cross-curricular theme in the National Curriculum – a vague and minimal direction, it must honestly be said, and a sad climbdown from when a future Conservative Secretary of State for Education, Mr Kenneth Baker, joined with me in presenting the Hansard Society's Report, *Political Education and Political Literacy* (Crick and Porter, 1978) (totally ignored by the Speaker's Commission, incidentally) to the then Labour Secretary of State, Shirley Williams, arguing wholeheartedly, or so it seemed, for its official adoption. None the less, the mere mention of 'citizenship' sensibly stimulated the Politics Association to seize the opportunity to issue a crisp, short leaflet, *Citizenship: The Association's Position*. It asked 'what should citizenship involve?' and gave short notes towards good answers under 'Knowledge' and 'Attitudes'; but on my marking would come down a class or two on 'Skills'. True 'participation in the democratic community' came under 'Attitudes' to be encouraged, but skills were all internalized towards readily commendable and respectable educational objectives, 'the ability to distinguish between fact and opinion', etc. So that while it spoke of the ability 'to evaluate differing views and arguments' as a skill, it did not speak of the ability to argue, to make an advocacy, to present a case; and the opportunity to speak about 'action skills' (an explicit category in the old *Hansard* report's specification of skills) was passed over. Perhaps I make too much of this. Perhaps just an omission in drafting? But in hard times it is not politic to trim the sails so much that the boat gets blown backwards. 'Politics', 'Citizenship', call it what you will, is a good educational subject; but it is more than a school educational subject. That is what is difficult about it. If it cannot reach outside at least it must point outside the classroom. That is what citizenship is about.

I am the ghost at this feast. Perhaps Banquo owes Lady Macbeth an apology for upsetting the guests and criticizing the family silver. I am vastly impressed by all the printed material produced . . . by the association to help teachers with the factual side of public examinations, also by how well the latest academic knowledge is being mediated into fifth and sixth forms, yet I am depressed to see how little material and thought has been produced for the rest of the school, for the earlier and the non-examination levels – those whom Lady Plowden once famously and simply called 'all our nation's children'. The journal has recently changed its name from *Teaching Politics* to *Talking Politics*. I see some gain for a particular constituency but a greater public loss.

To my recollection the motives of the founders of the Politics Association could be expressed under five heads: (i) to give comfort and companionship in adversity to, back then, some very isolated teachers; this has been well done; (ii) to provide practical help with teaching materials; this has been well done too, but mainly for those preparing for higher education, and some academic departments will often help sixth-form teachers, mainly because they want students; but they give little thought to educational values, the rest of the school or citizenship as the aim rather than political science; (iii) that materials and methods should engender political thought, not simply learning constitutional rules and institutional facts. This battle sways back and forth; when examination boards try to force thought by the strategy of real questions about real problems, memorizable cribs to

110

thoughtful-seeming answers are published (even by your-selves); (iv) to provide a bridge between secondary, further and higher education. It is my impression that the bridge to and from further education is in a bad state of repair (admittedly the opportunities are less); (v) to spearhead a crusade for citizenship education throughout the school. That was my primary motivation, and I suspect Derek Heater's, Ian Lister's and Alex Porter's too. This motivation now seems at rather low ebb – despite one shrewd and public-spirited protest by a member of your committee [Bernard Jones]: 'We must put more eggs in the basket of pre-sixteen education in order to legitimize our position, to help provide a teaching role for our members, to help provide future generations of graduates and teachers, and, of course, to fulfil our moral purpose.'

But times are inclement. Some public authorities are posi-tively hostile, unless citizenship can be redefined and debased to mean law-abiding good subjects either doing occasional voluntary service or gratefully receiving a 'citizens' charter' or placatory consumer rights. 'We are all here on earth to help each other', said the poet Auden, 'but what the others are here for, God only knows' – certainly not to be active citizens. Yet the educational and national need to ferment true participa-tive citizenship has never been greater.

7 In defence of the Citizenship Order 2000

> *We aim at no less than a change in the political culture of this country both nationally and locally: for people to think of themselves as active citizens, willing, able and equipped to have an influence in public life and with the critical capacities to weigh evidence before speaking and acting; to build on and to extend radically to young people the best in existing traditions of community involvement and public service, and to make them individually confident in finding new forms of involvement and action among themselves.*
>
> *Education for Citizenship and the Teaching of Democracy in Schools* (QCA, 1998)

The concept of citizenship and its history has in the last decade attracted much academic debate, debate often of a very high standard. Political thinking is not dead, but has locked itself up, or been locked up where it can do no harm, in the ivory tower. And although academic debate about the concept of citizenship almost always assumes the mantle of democratic principles and institutions and the practices of a free citizenry (I am not here concerned with what legal 'citizenship' means in autocracies and military dictatorships), there has been an astonishing lack of academic interest in Britain in what must be one of the essential conditions for the universal practices of free citizenship, education – specifically the period of compulsory school education of all our nation's children. There is an extensive educational literature on the provision and teaching of citizenship in schools (Heater, 1996; Ichilov, 1998; Hahn, 1998; *Oxford Review of Education*, 1999;

Torney-Purta *et al.*, 1999; Pierce and Hallgarten, 2000), but it is little used by students of politics in universities, indeed virtually unknown outside departments of education. Since 1986 we have had a compulsory National Curriculum for all local authority schools, but citizenship was not a required subject. Among official advisory papers on cross-curricular themes there was the excellent 'Education for Citizenship' (NCC, 1990), if any school cared to take it on; but few did in any systematic or intellectually coherent manner. What is surprising about the 1999 Citizenship Order was that it came so late on the scene and was not part of in the 1988 legislation. The then Secretary of State for Education, Kenneth Baker, was known to favour it. He was chairman of the Hansard Society when their *Political Education and Political Literacy* report was published (1978). He and I waited together on the then Secretary of State, Shirley Williams, to argue strongly for government money for in-service training, our clear priority. But being close to a general election she demurred and sent us away with funding for something less politically contentious, she said, that we had not asked for, research into assessment. It would not be proper for me to relate what he said to me as we left.

Perhaps in 1986 Baker judged that citizenship would have meant too much innovation and prescription all at once in the National Curriculum, or perhaps he was overruled by his Prime Minister. Who knows? But more fundamentally many leading politicians and also head teachers felt that there was no need for citizenship to be taught as a subject; all that was needed resided in the ethos of a good English school. The traditionalist version of this was, of course, an idealized picture of independent schools, and an outdated one at that – as I argued in Chapter 1.

Traditionalism stressed an ideal of *good* citizenship (obeying the law without question and giving up one's seat to elders on the underground) and progressivism an ideal of *active* citizenship (trying to change unjust laws, trying to democratize voluntary bodies, even the occasional demo and aggressive non-violent protest). Obviously I parody some well-known good intentions to argue that neither will do by itself, that both are needed in sensible combination. A new consensus that citizenship should be taught and learnt has come about as part of a general questioning whether our old institutions serve the purpose of our citizens – the population seen as an electorate; and worries about the alienation of young people from public values. Low voting turnout among the young is only one measure of this. To my mind, even more significant, is the low level of active participation of young people in voluntary bodies, even if they join. Yes, splendid examples to the contrary can be found, and they are heartening reminders of what is possible. But in number they disappoint grievously. Change will not come of itself.

In the 1970s some tried to promote programmes in schools with the object of enhancing what was cleverly called 'political literacy' – the knowledge, skills and values needed to be an informed, active and responsible citizen. The Hansard principles were beginning to catch on reasonably widely when the change of government in 1979 dampened such voluntary enthusiasms – at least after the going of Sir Keith Joseph who initially gave it some encouragement. But, in hindsight, it was always too narrowly political – or could encourage a narrowing sense of what counted as political: the activities of the parties, of the great and the good and of goings-on in Parliament. For 'political literacy' is needed in almost any form of group activity (a 'key skill'?), and even the skills needed for party or pressure group activity may best be learned in local voluntary groups and, indeed, in free discussions of real issues and the exercise of real responsibilities in school.

The terms of reference for the advisory group asked us 'To provide advice on effective education for citizenship in schools – to include the nature and practices of participation in democracy; the duties, responsibilities and rights of individuals as citizens; and the values to individuals and society of community activity.' It was the implications of

115

that last phrase that broadened the concept from political education into citizenship education. Some may suspect a mere politic play with words in this: surveys show that parents favour the idea of citizenship education (Institute for Citizenship, 1998) but perhaps not always 'political education'.

But there is classic political philosophy behind this shift. Did not de Tocqueville famously argue that the very foundations of liberty depend on 'corporations' or self-governing groups intermediary between the state and the individual? Edmund Burke extolled 'the small platoon' as a pillar of the state. An old eighteenth-century term of the Scottish enlightenment has recently been revived – 'civil society', what mediates between the individual and the state: vibrant in Western Europe, sadly lacking, diminished or destroyed in old countries of former Communist rule. And Aristotle had argued that if a tyrant was to be secure he must destroy all intermediary groups, because however unpolitical they were it was participation in such social groups that created mutual trust between individuals, without which any opposition to tyranny (or may one say to misgovernment in general?) is futile.

To come down to earth. There is now to be a new subject called 'Citizenship' in all secondary schools – statutory, therefore required and prescribed in an order. It rests on three practical ideals:

> Firstly, children learning from the very beginning self-confidence and social and moral responsible behaviour both in and beyond the classroom, both towards those in authority and towards each other … Secondly, learning about and becoming helpfully involved in the life and concerns of their communities, including learning through community involvement and service to the community … Thirdly, pupils learning about and how to make themselves effective in public life through knowledge, skills and values – what can be called 'political literacy', seeking for a term that is wider than political knowledge alone.
>
> (Advisory Group, 1998)

There is also to be a new non-statutory subject in primary schools, 'PSHE and Citizenship', for which authoritative guidance has been drawn up, not compulsory but likely to be taken seriously by the inspectorate, even when some schools are not enthused. But the advisory group were unanimous in wanting citizenship statutory in secondary schools. The history of take-up for the voluntary cross-curricular guidance papers has been derisive. Also the very idea of democratic citizenship is a universal one. So it must be a universal entitlement. Admittedly one can take a horse to water and it may not drink. But unless water is provided it cannot drink at all. The civic drink must be a universal entitlement, clearly there for all. The government has accepted that. If any ministers had doubts and might have thought that the Report's recommendations should be on offer to schools but not compulsory, three considerations prevailed. (i) Citizenship education in schools and FE colleges is a necessary condition for the success of constitutional reform, if part of its object is gradually to create a more participative, self-sustaining and genuinely democratic society. (ii) Citizenship education in schools and FE colleges is a necessary condition for a more inclusive society, or for helping to diminish exclusion from schools, cynicism, welfare-dependency, apathy, petty criminality and vandalism, and a kind of could-not-care-lessitude towards voting and public issues unhappily prevalent among young people. (iii) That, after all, we are a democracy, however imperfect, and its legal citizens should know how it works and how it could be improved if we could change our collective mentality from being subjects of the Crown to being both good and active citizens. All this is part of a liberal education.

The strong, bare bones of the Citizenship Order either directly follow from or are consistent with the main thrusts of the Report of the advisory group. Being a statutory order, that is to say a legally enforceable document, it contains only a formal statement of aims and only an implied justification; it carries no advice about the methods of delivery, learning techniques nor teaching methods appropriate to citizenship. That has come from the QCA, but very much, regarding the content, as guidance to other sources of guidance – the several leading citizenship NGOs. For official guidance will only be advice and guidance, and like the order itself, will not specify details of what is to be taught, and how. The virtue of the order is that the generality of its prescriptions will leave the school and the teacher with a good deal of freedom and discretion, more than in the other statutory subjects.

This has occurred, I think, for two reasons: firstly, it would not be appropriate for either the government (through the DfEE) or a central quango (the QCA) to give precise prescriptions on some politically or morally sensitive matters – the detail should be at arm's length from the state (it will be for Ofsted, LEA advisers and governors to watch for bias or bad teaching); and, secondly, in the very nature of citizenship (somewhat concerned with enhancing freedom, after all) there must be local discretion. Hence the order is 'a light touch order', or what I call 'strong, bare bones'. The schools will not be given ready-made lessons by either DfEE or QCA, nor told which 'events, issues and problems' should be discussed. If some teachers look for lessons off the peg, they will find a variety on offer from various independent bodies from which to pick and mix – notably the Citizenship Foundation, Community Service Volunteers (CSV), Council for Education in World Citizenship (CEWC) and the Institute for Citizenship. These are likely to be the main providers of beef on the bone, either in print or on their own Web sites or on the Citizenship branch of National Learning Web. Other bodies too will contribute on the parts of the order that touch on civil and human rights, race relations, sustainable development, global citizenship, constitutional reform, civil liberties, consumer rights and financial literacy. The order allows for considerable flexibility. What is not ruled in is not ruled out; therefore so long as everything in the order is covered to a basic level of understanding, such topics can be stressed more than others and used as gateways into the whole curriculum.

In the main the order follows the Report (to an unusual extent), even if the order as mandatory is terse and prescriptive whereas the Report offers justifications and explanations of its recommendations. The two must be read together, especially in relation to the teaching and discussion of 'events, issues and problems' – even if the Report says 'controversial' and the order less controversially says 'contemporary, issues and problems'. ('Does that worry you, Bernard?' 'Couldn't care less; teachers are not blind horses.') But in two respects the order goes radically further than the Report. The Report strongly recommended pupil participation both in school and in the local community as good practice, but not to be part of a statutory order – 'value-added' if you like. We thought we were being politically prudent – always a virtue in my book, quite literally (Crick, 1962). And the classroom curriculum was enough, we thought, for starters, being acutely aware both of the dangers of appearing to overload the bending backs of so many teachers and the difficulties of offering any national prescription on, say, the constitution and powers of school or year councils. But the Secretary of State sent word to the working party who were drafting the consultative order (civil servants, QCA, teachers, advisers) that actual participation could be mandatory, if we cared so to recommend. We did not demure. Colleagues were amused that for once I had been too politic and underplayed a strong hand. Half a cake would not have been better than none. Without the experiential, participative side of citizenship learning, some schools could turn (and still might if inspection does not follow the aims as well as the precise language of the order) the brave new subject into safe and dead, dead-safe, old rote-learning civics. So easily examinable. There is an awful lot that could be learnt about local government law. A recent book on education for participation begins by quoting a Yoruba proverb, 'the child carried on the back does not know the length of the road'. The editors wisely comment: 'The process of assisting children to become active citizens requires the teacher to keep a delicate balance between providing security and offering challenge' (Holden and Clough, 1998).

The aim of the new subject is to create active and responsible citizens. There is a philosophy behind the Report, of course: what scholars call civic republicanism, and also pluralism. These useful terms are not yet current in political and public discourse; perhaps citizenship education may change that. But 'civic republicanism' has nothing necessarily to do with 'no monarchy' – The Netherlands, Denmark and Sweden have monarchs but are noticeably more civic republican than, as yet, England – people there actually think of themselves as citizens. And 'pluralism' does not necessarily deny that in a legal sense the state is sovereign, but the theory asserts that the power of any state is necessarily both limited by and mediated through many powerful and varying group interests. Pupils must be encouraged (indeed each one of us – never too late to learn) to find and formulate their own values and group identities, but to recognize that in the United Kingdom (let alone Europe and the wide world beyond) there is a diversity of values – national, religious, regional and ethnic. Some of these we have in common, some not. We must learn to respect the values of all others equally, but respect neither implies agreement in everything nor equality of praise (Rawls, 1972; Runciman, 1966). In dealing with the young (even with students) we learn to correct error and work against all kinds of prejudice gently – but firmly, firmly but gently. As the jazzman said, 'Take it easy, but take it.'

The order, of course, applies only to England. But the curriculum it enjoins covers knowledge of the diversity of the four nations, the United Kingdom as a whole. If our children had some recognition from an early age that their England is part of a multinational United Kingdom, respect for other forms of diversity, religious and ethnic – so commonly misnamed racial – would be easier. What we have in common, what holds this diversity together, are the values and practices of a common citizenship. Yes, citizenship in schools needs to have a wide agenda. Its success will be difficult to measure for many years, for the real measures will not be assessments of performance in a subject matter, whether written or oral, but will be the consequences for social behaviour. This is neither easily measurable nor predictable in the short term. But it is common sense to make the big effort, at long last. We cannot any longer afford not to try. Within all our overall prosperity, something is rotten in the state of Denmark.

Why not be blunt – even if sheltering behind another's words? One of the shrewdest observers of English society has recently written:

> it is the main and inescapable business of an open democracy to control the natural impulses of capitalism, to turn them to its own purposes. The current myth, that unfettered capitalism will eventually raise the material standards of all, at no social cost but with greater social justice for all, is just that: a myth, a dangerous and damaging myth. A democracy may live with capitalism, but on its own terms, not those of capital. It does not have to be friends with capital; instead a wary relationship. (Hoggart, 1999)

I like 'wary relationship'. I think an education for citizenship should create some scepticism towards the state, but an informed scepticism. The philosopher George Santayana once said, 'Scepticism is the chastity of the intellect. One does not give oneself to the first set of new ideas that come along' – or to old ones for that matter. For scepticism is Hoggart's 'critical thinking', about everything we read and hear. Scepticism is not cynicism. Cynicism is the great enemy of the good society and what can rot the roots of education. 'They [teachers, social workers, politicians – whatever] are all the same. We're all just looking after ourselves. What the **** else is there?' But it is a poor and incomplete self that is not social. Our very self is a construct of how others see and react to us, which itself is a construct of how we see others, and how we are equipped to react to others. Is that not the true aim of education to be brought to recognize this? To be a good and active citizen is even helpful to the self.

121

8 Friendly arguments

Here are some edited extracts from addresses I have given
around some key aspects of the Report and in the
consultation period for the Citizenship Order. Sometimes I
have edited in as well as edited out. The first was on a
specific occasion, a conference on 'Values' called by the
Cook Foundation in 1998 in Glasgow, but I have taken in
some remarks on teaching citizenship through human
rights first made at a conference on human rights in
Birmingham that same year.

Values and rights are enough

I myself have, of course, objective values, you have sincere
opinions and they out there, all those *others*, have irrational
prejudices.

How simple if things were as easy as that. Actually I am,
like most of you, fairly sure of my own values – and of how
common they are; but I am often most puzzled what situations
it is appropriate to apply them to; particularly those situations
that appear to involve a conflict of values – for example (as
debated in yesterday's newspapers) a woman's right to choose
natural childbirth; but the risk to the life of her child if she
wilfully and ignorantly refuses Caesarean section when the
doctors say that the medical risk to the child is very high. That
is a more immediate and concrete case of two clear principles
conflicting (freedom of choice and the right to life) than the
perennial clash, made so famous among philosophers by the

late Isaiah Berlin, of liberty and equality (Berlin, 1958 and 1997) – a more unequal match nowadays in political practice than some moral and political philosophers and theologians have made it in theory.

My personal difficulty is that I do not believe that values can be taught – taught directly that is. They must arise from actual or imagined experience if they are to have meaning; or else they are but a set of rules to learn by rote. Children are clever little monkeys: if subject to discipline and if 'well taught' in a 'good school' with supportive parents they can rattle off definitions happily, starting if Christians with the Ten Commandments and ending with at least the highlights of the UN Declaration of the Rights of the Child, and can even pass exams or satisfy assessments on the meaning of values. But that all too often can be, if I may speak technically, what is called the 'in-one-ear-and-out-the-other' school of teaching; for after the assessment the mind is emptied in preparation for the next graded task.

Moral values must surely arise from experience if they are to enter into a person's character so that they as if instinctively influence behaviour. Recently I was in a primary school in the north of England in an absolute war zone. A majority of the children were from broken homes, nearly all from unstable homes with bad parenting – over 60 per cent on free school meals. But the school was an oasis of calm. The head said that it had helped that a father had beaten her up for stopping his daughter swearing, at which even that bad and sad non-community had rallied round: word had gone out that the school was not to be touched. Well, perhaps the head of the English inspectorate, Mr Chris Woodhead, is right: exceptional good teaching can make up for a poor environment – poverty is no excuse (but one cannot sensibly base policy on heroics; however, that's another argument). Certainly an almost heroic small band of teachers had achieved good results against the odds, in literacy and numeracy as well as social skills and values. But I doubt if he would have approved the methods.

A class of 6-year-olds was sitting on the floor in circle time when one little girl burst into tears triggering off another. The magic comfort bear was sent for from the head's room. Rather than dispute possession, they both hugged one side of it. 'What's wrong Mary?' Nothing was secret there. She sobbed out that her dad had been picked up the night before from the flat on a drugs charge resisting arrest. 'Was yer Mam with you?' No reply; another little girl piped up 'No, she works nights – on the game.' I suspect that in a 'good school' the teacher would have reproved that child, bundled the distressed one out of the room double quick and got back to the planned lesson. But she caught that ball and turned it into the lesson.

'Is it good to take drugs?', she asked the class. A unanimous roar of 'No' and cries of "tis wicked', 'dead wrong', 'them's bad'. These already streetwise children had been 'well taught', I thought cynically. But very well taught in fact, for the teacher pressed the loudest shouter, 'Why is it wrong, Tracey?' 'Cos it get you into trouble.' 'The police?' 'Aye the police; put me brither inside.' 'Be all right then if you weren't caught?' 'Nay, still be wrong.' 'Why?' 'Cos it mucks you up.'

I thought that was a good reply – she had said it was wrong (value statement, I am sure we all agree), but she could give two pragmatic reasons: one, the law, and the other personal responsibility. She was not just saying 'I fink; well it's my opinion, ain't it?' (the postmodernism of the streets). The teachers were demanding reasons, like in French schools, not just 'good' responses. But the teacher still did not let it rest. 'Just muck you up, Mary?' That was almost a question too far, for fighting tears the little girl said, 'Nay, 'ole family.' I truly felt that I was in at the birth of a class feeling the beginning of moral responsibility to others.

You can put that word responsibility into a good long list of moral or civic concepts to be learned. My citizenship committee has done so; and moreover helpfully construed three parts to both moral and political responsibility: care for others, premeditation and calculation about what effect actions are likely to have on others, and understanding of and care for the consequences. But responsibility needs anchoring in experience and the good teacher does not follow the curriculum slavishly but seizes just such opportunities as I was lucky to hear.

Please, I am not linking the need for values simply to problems in desperately deprived areas, despite the overwhelming need – as George Bernard Shaw long ago remarked – to make the poor and unemployed moral in case they hit back. Only that these things down there cannot be as easily masked as they usually are in the good behaviour of a good school. I wonder whether any teacher in Balerno High School – Balerno is a most expensive, beautiful and quiet suburb of Edinburgh – led a class discussion as to how three of last year's sixth form while still at school could have kicked to death in a drunken fight a boy from another school also in a good neighbourhood – all of them from conventional good homes? I am ungenerous enough to doubt if such a discussion would have taken place. Perhaps the head addressed the whole school solemnly at morning assembly – the 'water-off-a-duck's-back' and the 'now-that's-an-end-of-a-matter' theories of moral education.

I offer all this just as food for thought. Growing through circle time to adolescent and adult discussion, whether in school or on the street, the child has gradually to face that other people's values may differ and that our own values may often be in conflict with each other when facing practical problems. Telling the truth and compassion do not always walk hand in hand, just as exercising our rights does not always help the common good (for example, the paradox of the private motor car – do I have to explain? Well, freedom versus congestion). Or to take a deliberately provocative (of thought, not anger, I hope) example: punishment of violations of human rights does not always automatically override other values: compromises for the safety of the state can mean peace, security for the republic, life, liberty and the pursuit of happiness. Spain, South Africa, Chile – their compromises raise genuine clashes of values, irreconcilable simply by saying 'human rights' or 'justice'. Reinhold Niebuhr once wrote about 'Christian realism in politics' (Niebuhr, 1954).

Let me not be misunderstood. Citizenship and human rights *should* go together. Many have been teaching citizenship through human rights programmes, mostly very well devised. The Birmingham LEA has encouraged this for many years. But just remember that the idea of free citizenship preceded any clear idea of human rights. The idea of human rights arose first in the eighteenth century, long after the theory and practice of free citizenship was familiar. It extended the idea of citizenship to all, going with the idea of democracy, no longer a limited citizenry of the elite; but it also restrained democracy: not simply the rule of the majority, but a majority that had to be held to account, just as much as any autocrat or dictator, to ideas of the rights of man, that individual rights must be respected. And to remember that rights, whether set out in books, legislation or philosophic discourse, are human constructs, not found in nature, so always subject to debate and interpretation. 'Human rights' is a less arbitrary concept than 'natural rights'. Some want to extend the idea to almost everything they want or what they think others should want. This is plainly to debase the concept. The fewer rights we regard as basic the more powerfully can law and opinion form behind them. And to begin to talk about group rights is sometimes to raise awkward questions about how far certain groups claim rights *over* their individual members, typically to restrain them leaving the group or marrying out of it. Rights are a most powerful member of the class of values, but not necessarily decisive in every case.

The Citizenship Report dealt with these complex questions somewhat minimally by always linking rights with duties, or rights with responsibilities. My own favourite and somewhat dangerous way of drawing the clear moral distinction is to say 'Of course Salman Rushdie had a right to publish what might seem to the Muslim blasphemy, but was it morally responsible of him to do so?' Responsibility means thinking through the possible consequences of both actions and words.

The Report concluded a discussion of the history of the idea of citizenship: 'So our understanding of citizenship education in a parliamentary democracy finds three heads on one body: social and moral responsibility, community involvement and political literacy.' And of social and moral responsibility it said:

> This learning should be developed, not only in but also beyond school, whenever and wherever children volunteer, work or play in groups. Some may think this aspect of citizenship hardly needs mentioning; but we believe it to be near the heart of the matter. Here guidance on moral values and personal development are essential preconditions of citizenship. Some might regard the whole of primary school education as pre-citizenship, certainly pre-political; but this is mistaken. Children are already forming concepts of fairness, attitudes to the law, to rules, to decision-making, to authority, to their local environment and social responsibility etc. Also they are picking up, whether from school, home or elsewhere, some knowledge of whether they are living in a democracy or not, of what social problems affect them and even what different pressure groups or parties have to say about them. This can all be guided and built upon.

So 'values teaching' by itself is not enough for good citizenship. Those who say so are often confusing a precondition with an entailment, or a necessary condition with a sufficient condition. Knowledge and skills are needed as well as values, and from no set of values can one entail knowledge and skills without teaching them. Each is useless without the other. However, what is essential common ground is that at primary school 'circle teaching' or interactive and experiential teaching is practised for both PS-E and citizenship objectives – an essential way to fulfil the aims of both moral education and citizenship education. More traditional direct teaching may, indeed, be the best way forward to enhance literacy and numeracy. Neither PS-E nor citizenship teachers should or need to contest that for one moment. But both need to say very firmly that children learn responsibility best and gain a sense of moral values by discussing with good guidance from the earliest age real and controversial issues and by having opportunities to participate and take responsibility. Talk, discussion, debate and participation are the bases of social responsibility and intercourse and the grounding and practice of active citizenship. Simple and immediate issues get discussed at first, of course – home and neighbourhood, attitudes to stealing, etc., but then more complex social issues; with reasons and evidence for opinions being demanded at every stage.

Take the practical issues of drug and alcohol abuse, sexual morality and behaviour, and parenting. Each of these presumably begin with classroom discussions centred on personal responsibility – clearly PS-E territory in every sense; but in secondary school these issues will be also discussed as issues of public policy identified with parties and pressure groups, justice and law enforcement – more plainly citizenship.

Who is not aware of how ambivalent is public opinion, certainly as expressed in the Press? Demands are made that something must be done in schools, but alongside fears that the wrong things are being done; sometimes a naive belief that values can be directly taught, coupled with a somewhat contradictory fear of indoctrination. The view is even expressed that schools should keep out of both citizenship education and sex education because of fears of bias, so 'leave it to the parents'. Empirical research has shown how rarely the very parents who make such demands the loudest do, in fact, undertake such duties systematically, or at all. And then there are the parents who are either too busy or too ill educated themselves to educate their own children other than by example, sometimes good, sometimes not.

To put it logically: PS-E, RE, moral education, whatever we call education specifically for values, are necessary but not sufficient conditions for good citizenship and good behaviour. Individuals may have strong, good values; but their behaviour may be inept, at best, hostile at worst, when they encounter others with different beliefs. We do live in a multi-ethnic

129

society, and have been living in a multi-religious one for several centuries. And citizenship teaching not based on moral values and reasoning would either be mechanical and boring, or even dangerous – the apparent absence of values usually hides single-truth theories of value. Some values, however, like democracy itself and representation also, are specifically political. The word politics needs rescuing from its bad repute. That is what I tried to do long ago in a modern restatement of the Aristotelian tradition (Crick, 1962 and 1992). And political activity is too important to be left entirely to politicians. Political activity by citizens is the very essence of a free society. Sometimes politics needs rescuing from professional politicians necessarily concerned more with party unity and re-election than with educative public debate. But that is another big question.

However, that little group of 6-year-old girls I met in Newcastle did not need the concept of democracy to be well on the way to acting in the very earliest manner of democracies in the ancient world or in African village meetings – sitting in a circle and discussing earnestly a matter of common concern: 'Once yer starts yer can't kick it'.

Anti-racism should lead

Racism is the foulest blot on the human landscape. But it does not follow that a head-on charge against deeply entrenched positions is the most likely to be successful. The Macpherson Report on the Lawrence killing and the character of the police investigation recommended that 'anti-racism' should be taught in all schools and that a register should be kept and published of racial incidents. On first reaction the government seemed inclined to accept both these ideas, but cool heads soon saw that a published register would be a godsend for provocation by racist white youths. They would take a perverse pride in a high score for their school, or if a teacher did not report them, then a mate would complain to the governors. Simple.

To teach 'anti-racism' the draftsmen of the Citizenship Order chose a deliberately more subtle indirect route to the same end. 'Pupils should be taught about (a) the legal and human rights underpinning society and how they relate to citizens ... (b) the origins and implications of the diverse national, regional, religious and ethnic identities within the United Kingdom and the need for mutual respect and understanding.' These are the first two of seven 'should-be-taughts' under 'Knowledge and Understanding' for 14–16-year-olds in maintained schools. A similar formula appears for Key Stage 3. The order of words is deliberate. The theory is that if pupils can helped to see, not just in citizenship but through history, PSHE, RE, English and geography (and 'Sustainable Development') as well, that Britain has been a multinational state for a long time, also with real regional differences, and that once violent religious divisions are now mediated peacefully and tolerantly (with one obvious object lesson of the recent past in Northern Ireland seeming like the old history), it will then be easier to bring the racially prejudiced, firstly, into tolerance, then into acceptance and finally, hopefully, into mutual respect. Racial prejudice has to be combated, but skilfully and sensibly, not by beating the drum and direct assault, tactics seldom effective, often counter-productive, however much they seem to show pressure groups that 'something is being done'. Perhaps even to use the word 'race', however commonly and loosely it is used, is to perpetuate the racist belief that psychological characteristics are biologically determined rather than culturally, say ethnically (Hanniford, 1996). Even to talk of 'the equality of races' is a misleading, even a dangerous, way of talking about the equality of man and human rights.

Many working specifically in the field of race relations will differ, arguing that racialism because it's such an evil, so prevalent – albeit to differing degrees, such a denial of common citizenship and human rights, must be met head-on, even that it is the primary business of citizenship education when combined with the absolute centrality of human rights

(Ostler, 1992 and 1999). I understand this view, and many are deeply committed to it, morally, sometimes occupationally; but I think it is mistaken. The need for citizenship arises from far broader considerations than anti-racialism, and true citizenship has no place for racism and provides a secure framework against its recurrence; so to cure the disease itself as a denial of free and equal citizenship, not constantly to battle with the symptoms.

In this context a recent book by Yasmin Alibhai-Brown (Alibhai-Brown, 1999) is of unusual importance, based on two surveys commissioned by the IPPR (Institute for Public Policy Research) in 1997. In order to produce a government strategy to affect public attitudes towards ethnic communities in the UK, it is important to know what these attitudes are and how they have changed since the 1950s when substantial numbers of immigrants began to arrive from the ex-colonies. No comprehensive survey has been conducted since E. J. B. Rose's seminal *Colour and Citizenship* of 1966, despite all the huge bibliography one can find under 'race', 'colour' or 'ethnicity', words which are not synonyms (would journalists and students please note), still less to be lumped together under the label 'black' except in the rhetoric of both racists and of too many anti-racists. The first was a quantitative survey from NOP (National Opinion Polls) to find out the attitudes of white people by age and class towards Asian, Afro-Caribbean and Jewish peoples; and the second was a qualitative study by Opinion Leader Research to explore the reasons behind these largely negative attitudes. Ninety-four per cent of whites, for instance, believed that there was at least a little prejudice, with 46 per cent seeing it strong. Prejudice against intermarriage remains strong in all groups, actually stronger in the minority groups; but less strong among the young. The most common reason given for prejudice was economic and employment uncertainty – 'they take our jobs', etc.

These are just a few points. The author collects many other polls and surveys, and did some brave in-depth doorstepping research in trouble spots. The book is a solid compendium of up-to-date knowledge. But it is far more than that. What is truly impressive is the tone both of deep moral commitment and thoughtfulness, going together with, which is all too rare, a concern for practicality by setting down carefully, cautiously and sensitively, without rhetoric or hyperbole, what is known of the facts of the case. This is so unlike the perpetually strident tone of some leaders of anti-racist groups who, as if drunk with the righteousness of their cause and inflamed by flagrant, real injustices, lose all sense and perception of how to persuade those who need to be persuaded; at best they give fleeting comfort to their own communities, at worst their effectiveness is too often only that of the politics of institutional leadership within their own communities. Was it Orwell who said to Koestler, or Koestler to Orwell, 'Know thy enemy as thyself'? Polemicists all too often either speak to the saved already or speak simply to cheer their own. Anger is appropriate, but cool, considered and contemplative anger gets results, not the self-indulgence of hot rage. Alibhai-Brown explores seriously how to persuade the prejudiced, and to arouse the indifferent – matters not irrelevant to teachers.

She has no doubt, however, that the government itself must take the lead. Negatively, it must avoid making statements 'based on the assumptions that good race relations depend on tough immigration policies', and to avoid inflammatory language like 'bogus' and 'abusive' when characterizing those ineligible for refugee status under the already strict enough criteria of the Geneva Convention. Contradictory messages are common from different departments of government (that question of 'joined-up handwriting', as ever). Positively, the resources of government, so well developed to spin good news of the economy, the health service and education (sometimes a little ahead of hard truth), could be far better mobilized to spread news of positive achievements by groups and individuals in the minority communities, or of how proud we should all feel to have given succour to refugees from persecution. That is true common sense.

Alibhai-Brown gladly recalls Roy Jenkins's 'momentous speech' as Home Secretary (perhaps his 'finest hour'?) when he said that while integration was the goal, yet it did not mean

> the loss by immigrants of their own national characteristics and culture. I do not think we need in this country a 'melting pot' . . . It would deprive us of most of the positive benefits of immigration which I believe to be very great indeed. I define integration, therefore, not as a flattening process of assimilation, but as an equal opportunity, accompanied by cultural diversity in an atmosphere of mutual tolerance.

Certainly there are those who want to state an explicit duty to teach 'Anti-Racism' – multiculturalism is not enough. That is a temptation for Home Office ministers to endorse, perhaps not wholly conversant not so much with conditions in schools as with good practice in actual classroom teaching. But the thinking behind the multiculturalist approach of the Citizenship order has, I believe, two strong grounds, which the thrust of Yasmin Alibhai-Brown's argument shares – quite apart from her seeing that the priority must lie with example set by the government and prominent public bodies. The first is that explicit attacks on racism or teaching anti-racism full frontal can prove inflammatory – just what the racist white lads will look forward to in classroom discussion, or disruption. Indirect approaches may prove more effective in combating the fading but once real national prejudices (anti-Irishism, for instance), religious prejudices (anti-Catholicism of yore) and even to regional and class prejudices (take accent, for instance). Significant and hate-filled diversities are not all racial. Again, Northern Ireland (or the north of Ireland) reminds us of that. The second reason for an indirect strategy is the uncertainty principle: that we know little in general about what effect explicit strategies have and what training is needed – some evidence suggests that some methods can be counter-productive if applied to all the very different circumstances of each school's locality.

I have only one difficulty with the argument of this most judicious and ethically well-grounded book. It urges government to stress 'respect and acceptance rather than tolerance'. Charter 88 officials take this line too, objecting to 'toleration' being held up as a basic value of citizenship because it is 'condescending' to tolerate anyone. This view is common among the lobbies and leaders of ethnic minorities. However, we must distinguish. No one accepts everything and everyone as in every respect equal. We must discriminate, indeed, between good and evil, between practical and impractical policies. To discriminate as such is not wrong, only if for bad reasons; to tolerate is not to condescend, only if out of a false assumption of moral or social superiority. To tolerate is to recognize genuine differences, even to feel or state some disapprovals, but to limit one's reactions. Certainly I do not tolerate people because of their colour since the question does not arise for colour is morally irrelevant; I try to judge everyone as people, and their actions as good or bad, rarely wholly good or bad. But I do have to exercise toleration (that is to limit my disapprovals) of some people's religious and ideological beliefs, and of some of the practices that follow from them. I both disagree and disapprove, and of some other cultural practices too; but I restrain my behaviour while not abandoning my beliefs, nor expecting others to abandon theirs. I respect differences in a practical, peaceful, law-abiding way (hopefully). 'Respect' cannot mean that we think all sincere beliefs are equally true, or their consequences equally acceptable to all others in a society. The philosopher Ernest Gellner once said that it is imperative to be socially tolerant always, but intellectually tolerant never. We should not be ashamed of toleration as a prime value of freedom and civilization. Total acceptance would be the end of what we all are, significant differences as well as rights and humanity in common. We should be far more conscious of being a multi-cultural society and a multinational state. To demand full acceptance rather than toleration is to demand assimilation rather than integration, a single common culture rather than, what we have long had, a pluralistic society. The practices of a common citizenship hold together real differences of national, religious and ethnic identities to the mutual advantage of minorities and majorities alike.

World citizenship comes first

The Citizenship Order for Key Stage 3 sets out the 'Knowledge and Understanding' pupils should be taught under nine headings, of which the last is: 'the world as a global community and the political, economic, environmental and social implications of this, and the role of the European Union, the Commonwealth and the United Nations'. And for KS4 out of ten prescriptions the last two are: '(i) the United Kingdom's relations in Europe, including the European Union, and relations with the Commonwealth and the United Nations. (j) the wider issues and challenges of global interdependence and responsibility, including sustainable development and Local Agenda 21'. And in the 'Programme of Study' KS3 pupils are to learn 'further about the key concepts, values of dispositions of fairness, social justice, respect for democracy and diversity; through study which covers issues at a range of levels, for example, school, local, national and global; and through learning in the community'.

Some organizations, like the Council for Education in World Citizenship (CEWC), Oxfam and the United Nations Association have developed excellent model citizenship curriculums or activities, premised on the concepts of 'global citizenship' or of 'world citizenship'. They must be disappointed both at the baldness of these references, and at the deliberate order of words in 'school, local, national and global'. They have worked with many teachers who have caught the imagination of young children, even or especially in primary schools, and brought them into an interest in citizenship by introducing them either to global environmental problems (thus fitting in nicely with ideas of 'sustainable development' as a cross-curricular theme) or by studying the life and problems of a Third World country or region. Begin with the globe and work into the neighbourhood. But the Citizenship Order and the QCA guidance deliberately point in the other direction. Teachers must reach the globe (both to feel moral concern and to understand what 'interdependence' means), but by beginning with what is immediately familiar.

Disappointment at the baldness of the references I have already explained, indeed extolled the virtues of what David Blunkett calls a 'light touch order' and I gloss as 'strong bare bones'. This is freedom from excessive central direction − freedom, more freedom at least than in other statutory subjects. It is for these worthy bodies, very like organizations for human rights or with human rights programmes, to continue to offer schools a choice of good materials and ideas for good practice to put flesh on the strong bare bones. *So long as the whole curriculum is covered* (or to follow QCA's guidance for PSHE and citizenship in primary schools), it is flexible enough for different emphases in different schools. So nothing that has and is working well need be abandoned. (I stress coverage because sometimes in recent years it was easier, less contentious, to teach about problems in the big wide world than those closer to home.)

There is a deeper intellectual reason, however, why some of the global-first organizations and teachers must always remain a little disappointed. This has never been put more clearly than by Hannah Arendt:

Nobody can be a citizen of the world as he is the citizen of his country. [Karl] Jaspers, in his *Origin and Goal of History* (1953), discusses extensively the implications of a world state and a world empire. No matter what form a world government . . . might assume, the very notion of one sovereign force ruling the whole earth, holding the monopoly of all means of violence, unchecked and uncontrolled by other sovereign powers, is not only a forbidding nightmare of tyranny, it would be the end of all political life as we know it. Political concepts are based on plurality, diversity and mutual limitations. A citizen is by definition a citizen among citizens of a country among countries.

137

His rights and duties must be defined and limited, not only by those of his fellow citizens, but also by the boundaries of a territory. Philosophy may conceive of the earth as the homeland of mankind and one unwritten law, eternal and valid for all. Politics deals with men, nationals of many countries and heirs to many pasts; its laws are the positively established fences which hedge in, protect, and limit the space in which freedom is not a concept but a living political reality. (Arendt, 1970, p. 84)

Not for one moment am I confusing CEWC, Oxfam and the United Nations Association with the erstwhile World Government Movement (which Laski famously said 'stands with both feet firmly planted in mid-air'); nor am I denying, indeed I strongly affirm, the moral inspiration and thrust of their work. The crucial test of ethical values is that they apply to strangers, and those afar, not only those in our midst. And intellectually we must grasp the interdependence of all countries, for prosperity, for culture and most urgently to prevent the further and most threatening degradation of our globe's environment. There are limits to free trade, which must concern us all. All markets need regulating, even or especially global markets. But I am against intellectual confusion, especially when it may lead to a lack of realism in persuading our young to consider problems in some immediately perceived and sensible order of priorities. 'A citizen is by definition a citizen among citizens of a country among countries.'

School governors, another task

If David Blunkett was to fulfil the intention of the White Paper of 1997, *Excellence in Schools*, 'to strengthen education for citizenship and democracy', he had little choice but to propose citizenship as a statutory subject. For the history of cross-curricular guidance papers had not been a happy one – as was seen at once by the advisory group who reported last year on *Education for Citizenship and the Teaching of Democracy in Schools*. My own views on the coming of a National

Curriculum are by now both irrelevant and private, but there was little choice, in the context of an established National Curriculum, to which both main parties were committed, but to go the whole way to achieve David Blunkett's long premeditated ambition: so to make it a statutory subject. What is not legally required and not assessed is too often not taken seriously, by teachers and pupils alike. Under Kenneth Baker an excellent guidance paper was issued by the old National Curriculum Council on 'Education for Citizenship' (1990), but to be fair to him, no one realized at the time how ineffective guidance papers would be in a crowded curriculum increasingly subject to publicized measurement of (measurable) results. The advisory group, which included Lord Baker, was unanimous and quick to decide that we would be wasting our time with anything other than a recommendation that it should be statutory in secondary schools.

Governors, advisers and head teachers will notice two things, however, that are bound to affect their work. Firstly, that it is education for citizenship that is being proposed, not just for political literacy: gaining a knowledge of, as well as the skills to volunteer and work in, community organizations, as well as in those more overtly political; and even in voluntary bodies, political skills can be useful – to understand what are the purposes of an organization, and to be able to contribute towards and shape its policies. Secondly, because the new subject is, what Blunkett likes to call 'a light touch order' it neither prescribes precisely what should be taught nor how it should be taught. It is based more on the idea of 'learning outcomes' than on precise prescriptions as to how to reach them. Most of the Press has missed this, indeed missed how much nearly all of the 'minor' changes in the whole National Curriculum move in this same direction. But, of course, more freedom for the school and the teacher in an admittedly sensitive area, especially in the early years of the new subject bedding down, as it were; so this may involve yet more need for governors to mediate between the school, parents and public bodies.

The Citizenship Order is unique, however, among subject orders in putting considerable stress on discussion – informed and exploratory discussion. For all the great importance of numeracy and literacy, what teacher trainers awkwardly call 'oracy' (i.e. coherent human speech) is equally important. Most decisions, reports and first impressions are made that way. Pupils are directed 'to study, reflect upon and discuss significant aspect of some topical political, social and moral, issues, problems and events'. Those words are carefully chosen: parties and the media make *issues* but there are some perennial *problems* which they can neglect or avoid; and *events* allow teachers on occasion to postpone that carefully prepared lesson to catch the pupils' interest in an event of the day.

But, of course, open-ended discussion can lead to misunderstanding, among pupils, parents and Press about what is being taught. Fundamentally, it is a process of civilized discussion and critical examination that is being taught, but misunderstanding can easily arise at first that it is one particular striking or memorable opinion (among others) in a discussion that is being taught. In the advisory group's report there was a whole section on 'Guidance on the Teaching of Controversial Issues' which should not get lost, and a briefer summary in the QCA's Guidance on Citizenship. No issues are ruled in (despite too many lobbies to be specifically mentioned), but no issues are ruled out. So some issues are bound to be discussed that some people will inevitably think should not be discussed at all, despite their presence in newspapers, radio and television. The 1996 Education Act already requires discussions of political matters to be balanced (as in the Broadcasting Acts), and it specifically proscribes partisan teaching. But choice of issues is left free, so head teachers and governors will have to sort out locally protests by pressure groups and some parents against certain topics being discussed at all – no central direction to fall back on. My view is that it is common sense that if issues are widely discussed in the media, they should be sensibly discussed in school; preparation for adult life, indeed. To recall again that recent anthology on pupil participation quoting a Yoruba saying: 'a child carried on the back does not know the length of the road'.

Among the Attainment Targets pupils are to 'participate effectively in school and community-based activities, demonstrating a willingness and commitment to evaluate critically such activity' – so few words, but such a major implication. Schools are now required to organize 'community-based activities', as some but not all have been doing for a long time. The inspectorate are unlikely to be happy with simply a token visit once a year to a session of the local Council; that would be out of step with the requirement to prepare for active citizenship – the constant reiteration of 'good citizenship' and 'active citizenship'. Here governors can play a key role in acting as go-betweens for community organizations, local business and schools. The Citizenship Coalition (which links the main charities assisting citizenship learning in schools) are advocating the establishment of Community Citizenship Forums for this purpose.

Universities could help

What effect may this have on the universities? I see some small but interesting short-term effects but potentially much larger long-term effects. The short-term effect will mainly affect social science departments, with more students in school or colleges taking relevant A levels. I pick my words carefully, for as soon as one grasps the remit set by David Blunkett that my committee followed, one sees that it is not just political studies that will be enhanced: 'To provide advice on effective education for citizenship in schools – to include the nature and practices of participation in democracy; the duties, responsibilities and rights of individuals as citizens; *and the value to individuals and society of community activity.*'

I italicize those last words because no existing A levels or GCSEs in either sociology or political studies have that kind of recommended emphasis: in addition to political and economic

141

literacy, learning about local and national voluntary bodies, and the interaction between them and local public services. Between the state and the individual there is the community, whether as a reality or as a quasi-ideal concept of the arena for a socially responsible and decent life. Although the Citizenship Order only applies to compulsory schooling up to 16, post-16 exams are likely to become more general than the present (in my considered opinion) overspecialized and over-academic political studies and sociology syllabuses. And it would be odd if the government thought that education for citizenship should stop at 16! Not to stretch my own memory overmuch, broader citizenship exams will make university first-year teaching in the social sciences both more rigorous and easier for the teacher: no longer half the customers knowing nothing and the other half thinking, often mistakenly, that they know it already.

There may be other incidental benefits, jobs. It will soon be easier for social science graduates to get accepted for initial teacher training. At present lack of a National Curriculum subject counts heavily against them. This could at least be some contribution to the acute shortage of teachers (even if we can all think of bigger contributions, such as attractive salaries and trying to create a sense of the status of teachers closer to that in Germany, France, The Netherlands and the Scandinavian democracies). Of course already the new universities (formerly polytechnics) commonly have less specialized degree structures which are that much more relevant to teacher training. But should we not follow some German universities and, amid all those eclectic final year options in a typical social science degree structure, offer one on citizenship education? It could be interesting to consider both the basic presuppositions of the discipline and how it can be simplified and taught at different levels – at least as a tempter, a taster, possibly linked to some work experience in local schools. This might help to break down barriers between departments of education and disciplinary departments.

When it was clear that the Report was broadly accepted, I

had the polemical pleasure of reminding the two professional bodies much concerned – the Politics Association in schools and the Political Studies Association in universities – that any triumphalism about a Citizenship Order is out of place. For two good reasons: that 'Citizenship', both as a practice and a subject is, indeed, a much wider concept than the present discipline and may benefit and influence sociology equally; and that neither the government nor the public are likely to thank universities for judging everything in schools in terms of recruitment fodder for existing subject and syllabus demarcations. Matters of wider public interest are involved.

For too long in England we have been basically a deferential, subject culture, not a citizen culture. If this is a platitude, it needs making pregnant with real meaning. The Citizenship Report stated, boldly and calmly: 'We aim at no less than a change in the political culture of this country both nationally and locally: for people to think of themselves as active citizens, willing, able and equipped to have an influence in public life and with the critical capacities to weigh evidence before speaking and acting.' 'Words are lightly spoken', as the poet said. But consider what might be the effects on the universities when a generation enters university, not just as students but, in another half decade, as potential young teachers, who have already gained some of the skills, knowledge and values associated with the great tradition of citizenship and free government. Learning and the advancement of knowledge would not be threatened. Some universities have held out against excessive government-led passions for an economic, utilitarian justification for almost everything, coupled with beliefs that nothing is meaningful that cannot be measured. They have held out with difficulty, sometimes with ignominy and deceit, but held out still to a surprising extent (in most places) nevertheless. But if a citizenship culture was to grow, alongside vocationalism, balancing, modifying and amending it, this would create a realization that universities are all in some measure part of other communities, and have educational responsibilities to communities, local as well

143

as national. The new 'mentoring' scheme to bring under-graduates into schools for a few hours' paid tutoring is an imaginative straw in the wind.

Citizenship education in schools can not, of course, have any great transforming effect on its own. But it is not on its own. Even if the present government is, as yet, better at illuminating some capital letters than at joined-up hand-writing, yet the idea of a far wider participative citizenship is beginning to be seen as an essential condition both for constitutional reform and for attempts to make voluntary and local bodies more powerful and effective in delivering both local and national policy and services, mediated to local conditions. The BBC has grasped in several new educational ventures that citizenship is a matter for the whole of society. As yet, too many contradictions: just as in Thatcherism, the state trying get out of things can actually strengthen central power. Economic restraints, real, residual or perceived as politically prudent, still severely limit local initiatives and the delivery of ideas of democracy and community that the government wants to make common coin. The continued governmental distrust of local authorities is not entirely helpful.

These contradictions are very evident in the university sector. So much funding simply follows measurable produc-tivity, multiplying useless and needless publication of articles, the majority of which are rarely read by anybody, as if every teacher had to be, or pretended to be, an original scholar. And now there is little funding for extramural teaching, such departments diminished or collapsing all over the country; for funding now overwhelmingly favours vocational, certifi-cated courses. Those in the community who value education for its own sake and non-vocational study are now left out in the cold, or charged 'the real cost' which excludes much real need. Lifelong learning does not mean a multiplication of qualifications. None the less, a cultural change is taking place and may soon be government-led – as in this small matter with big implications of citizenship teaching in schools: if not the equality of income redistribution, certainly the relative equality of a democratic and participative culture. Concern for helping, relating to and studying local communities will soon begin to modify the excesses of the vocational, predominantly economistic thrusts of the Thatcher years. Universities are part of society and, in both senses of the word, a critical part which should be playing a major role in the wider objectives of creating a citizenship culture. I am now far from alone in arguing this (Annette, 1999; Buckingham-Hatfield, 2000).

9 The presuppositions of citizenship education

This is a lightly revised version of an article which appeared in *The Journal of the Philosophy of Education of Great Britain*, **33**(3), 1999, and was originally the opening lecture at the annual conference of the Society for the Philosophy of Education at New College, Oxford, Easter 1999. I thank the editor for permission to reproduce it here.

Let us go back to the very beginning of discourse about citizenship and education. Aristotle reasoned that to be a good man one must also be a good citizen, even if he admitted that it was possible to be a good citizen without being a good man. But Benjamin Constant drew a mordant distinction in his once celebrated essay 'The Liberty of the Ancients Compared with that of the Moderns':

> The aim of the ancients was the sharing of social power among the citizens of the same fatherland: this is what they called liberty. The aim of the moderns is the enjoyment of security in private pleasures; and they call liberty the guarantees accorded by institutions to these pleasures.

Even in our yet more modern or postmodern era these liberties are now guaranteed by the United States of America enforcing on the rest of the world a free-market economy (except when it touches some of their own domestic interests).

A recent writer, Mark Philp, in an essay on 'Citizenship and

147

Integrity' (Philp, 1999, pp. 19–21), has said that it is not difficult to see the attraction of citizenship in the classical mode: 'the vision of a virtuous, active citizenry, engaged in deliberation on the proper ends of their association and taking turns at ruling and being ruled – especially when coupled with the assumption that civic virtue provides the natural completion of the broader moral virtues'. Something of this ancient ideal is a presupposition of democratic states when they command or influence the content and manner of educational systems. But we have to admit, says Philp, that this noble view 'has little moral significance for most people' – and who can disagree? For it is not merely that many people can live a purely self-centred life, almost entirely dominated by acquisition, sport and good or bad sex, well protected by a liberal state, but that claims can be made that the private life is more virtuous than that public life as pictured by Aristotle and, in our times, by Hannah Arendt, in her way, or by John Dewey, in his. Philp embarrasses my thesis by quoting my favourite humanist author to this narrowing effect. For said Montaigne:

> Storming a breach, conducting an embassy, ruling a nation are glittering deeds. Rebuking, laughing, buying, selling, loving, hating and living together gently and justly with your household – and with yourself not getting slack nor betraying yourself, is something more remarkable, more rare and more difficult. Whatever people say, such secluded lives sustain in that way duties which are at least as hard and as tense as those of other lives.

So the case for active adult citizenship should not be overstated. It cannot be made universal by persuasion nor compulsory by law. If made compulsory, it is either trivial – say that voting is compulsory (then we all have heard what many Australians write on their ballot paper), or it is ideological and intense – as in one-party states and in regimes of ultranationalism; not what we mean by liberty in any good sense.

However, to put it simply, a state that does not have a

tradition of active citizenship deep in its culture or cannot create in its educational system a proclivity to active citizenship, that state is running great risks. Do, or you will be done by. The extreme risk is, of course, lack of support in times of war or in times of economic crisis, but the more obvious risks are lawlessness within society; perhaps not general but at least that sections of young people feel alienated, disaffected, driven to or open to strong degrees of antisocial behaviour.

Nearly everywhere there is citizenship education in schools – say in every country in the European Community (including now, or very soon, last of all as usual, England), the United States, Canada, Australia, New Zealand – some historically contingent sense of crisis has been the trigger, not a reflection that knowledge of the political and social institutions of a country should be a normal entitlement of children growing towards an all too adult world. That events seem to drive rational reflection is an ironic tribute to the intense traditionalism of most educational systems and what are believed to constitute proper subjects and proper ways of learning – as if the great political and social philosophers had never existed: Aristotle, Machiavelli, Hobbes, Rousseau, Montesquieu, Kant, Hegel, Mill, de Tocqueville, Marx, Durkheim, Weber, Arendt, Aron, Popper . . .

The calmer view of a deliberate education for citizenship might be that since politics, rather like sex, cannot be avoided, indeed civilized life depends on it, on them, then it had better be faced. Since it cannot be avoided, care and time should be given to it. And since it is an interesting subject, it should be taught in an interesting manner. Civilized life and organized society depend upon the existence of governments, and what governments should do and can do with their power and authority depends, in turn, both on the political structure and beliefs of inhabitants and groups within society. To take a Greek or a Jacobin view of the matter may now appear to go too far: that man is only properly man if she or he is also a citizen active in public life [Crick, 1962]. But it remains true that a man is still regarded as less of a man when he or she has no 'public spirit', has no concern for and takes no part in all the jostlings of self-interest, group interests and ideals that constitute a political society (often loosely or optimistically called a democratic society). Only a few would maintain that the good life for all or most consists in the avoidance of public concerns; but nearly all would recognize that our whole culture or style of life is less rich, that is less various and shapely, and is less strong, that is less adaptable to change and circumstances, if people of any age group believe that they should not or cannot influence authority. Feelings of help-lessness to have any effect create a widespread could-not-care-lessitude, if not a potentially corrosive cynicism.

These may sound like abstract generalities, but the implica-tions for education are embarrassingly concrete. Any worth-while education must include some explanation and, if necessary, justification of the naturalness of politics: that men both do and should want different things, indeed have differ-ing values which are only obtainable or realizable by means of or by leave of the public power. So pupils must both study and learn to control, to some degree at least, the means by which they reconcile or manage conflicts of interests and ideals, even in school. Michael Oakshott's radical scepticism that politics is simply keeping a ship afloat on a voyage with no predeter-mined destination and that therefore it cannot be learned from a book but only from experience (Oakshott, 1962, pp. 111–36), is at least half-right; but it is also half-wrong, for the conservative and the progressive should both come together (and perhaps Rousseau is their go-between) to see that a strong experiential element is needed in an education for politics, but so is some knowledge of institutions and history (or in terms of Oakshott's metaphor, of navigation). It seems, to use one of his own favourite concepts, a somewhat arbitrary arrest of experience to make a sharp, even an absolute division, between schooling and adult experience, and to limit – for this must follow – those fit to govern to those brought up amid a class of people experienced in governing.

The point of departure, however, is all-important. When we

ask for directions, there are occasions on which we should receive the famous reply of the English rustic when asked the way to Biddecome [*sic*]: 'I would not start from here if I were you.' In practice we have to start from where we are: perhaps as an inhabitant of a state that conceives politics as neither subversive nor divisive, nor yet as the implementation of a single and authoritative set of ideological or patriotic truths which are to be extolled but not questioned. But in education in a reasonably free society (and education in its full sense can only exist in reasonably free societies), we are reasonably free, despite practical limitations of various kinds, to start from where we choose. So we should start with politics itself. If we start from some other point, some of these conventional and innocent-sounding points of departure (such as I have discussed earlier) like 'the constitution' or 'good citizenship' or 'reform' or even 'human rights', we could risk either heading off in the wrong direction entirely or creating a positive distaste for or resistance to part of the journey.

Let me give a personal example of some public interest. When I came to the first meeting of the advisory group on the Teaching of Citizenship and Democracy in Schools, I was worried that some of the committee might want to limit a new curriculum to the teaching of what used to be called civics – the facts about institutions, respectable fantasies about the universal good work of elected representatives, both local and national, and learning about the British constitution – despite the obvious difficulty that we Brits do not have one; or if there is, I admit, a sense in which we do, then defining it is a matter of partisan dispute – an 'essentially contestable concept' indeed.

A civics curriculum would have proved a Greek gift to teachers. Such could easily make matters worse if constitutional platitudes of the 'our glorious Parliament' kind were to be thrust on an already sceptical youth to instil only boredom mitigated by contempt. But I misjudged my committee. They all settled for something realistic, down-to-earth, that focuses on citizenship and politics as participative and controversial matters, aiming to discuss and explore the diversity of values and interests that exist in a pluralistic society. If in addition as part of a curriculum (the blessed mantra of 'values, knowledge and skills') we did recommend something 'civic', it was not just knowledge of political and legal institutions but also of all the voluntary groups and pressure groups in a school's neighbourhood that a child could encounter, should encounter and should be encouraged to participate in; to form dispositions that would put knowledge to use.

The strategy of 'learning outcomes' we recommended was to give the teachers substantial freedom as to how to achieve them, not detailed prescriptions of content. Such freedom is part of the tradition of free citizenship.

Many or most of the outcomes in my report's recommendations took the form of concepts. I believe that all education, whether in school or out of school, consists of increasing an initial understanding of language and increasing ability to use it to adjust to more complex external relationships and events, to extend one's range of choice within them and finally, in the case of citizenship, to influence them. At all times we have some general image of the world in which we live, some understanding however tentative, primitive or even false, and the slightest degree of education consists in forming explanations of these images or offering generalizations, however simple, about alternative images or modifications of early ones, with some argument or some appeal to external evidence. The images are composed of concepts. Whether they are aware of it or not, children begin with concepts and they and we try to sharpen them, to extend their meanings to see links between them, and then to go on to invent or accept special sets of concepts for new experiences and problems.

Thus there is not really a choice about beginning with concepts. The real choice is between beginning with the concepts of a theoretical discipline and simplifying them – as my old collaborator Derek Heater in the 1970s seemed to suggest, following Jacob Bruner; either that or to begin in each school empirically with the actual usage of those whom a teacher is trying to teach. Shall I say the demotic rather than the structured?

'People do not first make generalisations and then embody them in concepts,' wrote Peter Winch (Winch, 1958, p. 58), 'it is only by virtue of their possession of concepts that they are able to make generalisations at all.' And a thoughtful contemporary political philosopher, Sheldon Wolin, wrote:

> The concepts and categories that make up our political understanding help us to draw connections between political phenomena; they impart some order to what otherwise might appear to be a hopeless chaos of activities; they mediate between us and the political world we seek to render intelligible; they create an area of determinate awareness, and thus help to separate the relevant phenomena from the irrelevant.
>
> (Wolin, 1960, p. 21)

But a warning, and from a powerful source: 'One should never quarrel about words,' argued Karl Popper (Popper, 1963, p. 93); definitions do not settle arguments and important concepts cannot be defined too precisely. What we are really interested in, our real problems, are factual problems, or in other words, problems of theories and their truth. Certainly this is a proper warning against a sterile linguistic approach, as if ultimately a good dictionary could settle disputes, or as TV panelists say, 'Well, personally I define democracy as everyone getting on with their own thing.' But theories are built out of concepts. Concepts are our primary perceptions of a field of cognate problems. 'Problems first' is Popper's proper and real exhortation to the scientist, including the social scientist. But the teacher must be concerned with establishing and refining actual usage and usages before he or she can consider problems, generalizations, evidence and truth. And to the teacher of citizenship Popper's advice can be politically dangerous, unless he or she can first establish if not objective, then at least rationally defensible procedures for selecting which problems to introduce and discuss. None the less, the

Popperian point is to be taken seriously: the object of the journey is not to learn to speak proper, but to understand and explain general relationships; and also to understand the probable consequences of following inferences drawn from one set of values rather than another.

Ernest Gellner made much the same point in reproving Peter Winch for his Wittgensteinian belief (arrogance?) that to understand the concepts of a society is to understand the institutions of that society:

> Concepts and beliefs are themselves, in a sense, institutions among others; for they provide a fairly permanent frame, as do other institutions, independent of any one individual, within which individual conduct takes place. In another sense, they are correlates of *all* the institutions of a society: and to understand the *working* of the concepts of a society is to understand its institutions.
> (Gellner, 1973, p. 49)

It is, indeed, by the *working* of concepts that one understands a society; thus we need to start with explicating meanings of such concepts as 'power' and 'authority', *inter alia*, not to show their true meaning, but the role the terms play in, for instance, different political doctrines (Conservative, Liberal and Socialist theories of each) and in different kinds of social or professional groups. Ian Lister puts the matter moderately but forcefully: 'although a command of the vocabulary of political education is not the same thing as a political education, it is part of it. In the beginning was the thing, but we cannot analyze the thing without concepts' (Lister, 1987, p. 32).

Stephen Toulmin said in his monumental *Human Understanding* (Toulmin, 1972, p. 35): 'What are the skills or traditions, the activities, procedures instruments of Man's intellectual life and imagination – in a word the *concepts* – through which that human understanding is achieved and expressed?' And he coins the epigram: *each of us thinks his own thoughts; our concepts we share with our fellowmen.* Certainly a private concept, unintelligible to others, would be no use as a concept. Concepts are not true or false, they are simply public and useful. The concepts of political and social life need simplifying for pupils, not complicating. I say this as a cheerful challenge to the assembly of born-again complicators in academic political philosophy, who never reach the schools, the press or the public.

We go wrong at the beginning of complicated enterprises. Any learned fool can elaborate in a PhD or treatise. It needs a certain brave simplicity to begin at the beginning. Collingwood warned us in *The Idea of History* that all too often we are reading answers to questions that are never stated. My main prejudice was to begin at the beginning, that is to build a citizenship teaching relevant to all the school population from concepts that children actually hold or that are least familiar to them. I am under no illusions at all that such a set of concepts, however elaborated, refined and criticized, would be likely to remain adequate for an understanding of the real political world unless supplemented by concepts suggested, introduced or taught (what you will) from elsewhere. And I am under no illusion that, alas, apart from the common sense and common experience of teachers, there is any great knowledge of these primary concepts anywhere. Too much of political socialization research turns out simply to be over-structured investigations of the attitudes of schoolchildren to adult political concepts: there is too little on the political language and lore of schoolchildren, there is no political Piaget. More research is needed in this area – if only to be able to check our common-sense view as to what terms like 'fair' and 'authority' mean to the children when we start teaching. Half the battle in education at any level is knowing the preconceptions of the pupils by listening intelligently.

In the Hansard Society report of 1978, *Political Education and Political Literacy*, some of us were bold enough to propose twelve basic concepts for a teacher of citizenship [see Chapter 5 above]: a vocabulary adequate for a basic understanding of the political world – give or take synonyms and negations, of course. I won't weary you by attempting to justify that speculative escapade, which could have formed no part of a report to government, nor an order based on that report – though something like it could form part of semi-official and unofficial guidance papers to follow.

However, one idea I want to keep alive or revive: that the very project of a free citizenship education, as distinct from an indoctrinatory one, whether ideological or simply patriotic, must be based on a limited number of presuppositions that we called in the old Hansard report, *procedural values*: Freedom, Toleration, Fairness, Respect for Truth, Respect for Reasoning. Different substantive values are to be discussed, rarely resolved; but such discussions must be based on presupposed ways of proceeding.

Freedom

Political freedom is the *making* of choices and doing things of public significance or potentially public significance in a self-willed and uncoerced way. This is not merely a basic concept and a value, it is in a formal sense a procedural value, for without freedom there can be neither knowledge of nor voluntary participation in politics. True, some regimes deny freedom and thus knowledge of politics is low, but even the secret writing or the *samizdat* are some sign of freedom, however minimal, of potential importance. But to conceive of a political education that did not seek to maximize freedom would be paradoxical.

I prefer to say 'freedom' rather than 'liberty' simply because it has a more positive connotation. We speak of a free action, never action in liberty. English, unlike French or German, enables us to make this distinction clearly: freedom is a status linked to the potential for activity, whereas liberty is simply being left alone. Freedom suggests not merely being at liberty from specified restraints and interventions, but being free actually to choose between alternatives. 'They are perfectly at liberty to complain', is usually a very qualified truth, whereas 'they are acting much too freely' or even 'abusing their freedom', may well be true, but it does imply action. Easier in practice to restrain excess than to try to arouse habitual passivity. Liberty can be potential or on licence, but freedom is an activity. I think that Isaiah Berlin confused this point in his famous essay *Two Concepts of Liberty* (Berlin, 1958; and Crick, 1968). But he was right to stress that no one value is an end in itself, however, or automatically overrides all other values. Freedom is to be encouraged, and tested by whether it is exercised; but it will be limited by other values. So if freedom is a component of political literacy, it carries an image of use about it, not simply learning how our glorious liberties were preserved for us by well-meaning gentlemen in the good old days. There is small but rather important inference for teaching practice: pupils as well as teachers must have some freedom to choose what issues to explore and discuss.

Toleration

Toleration is the degree to which we accept things of which we disapprove. It is often confused with permissiveness. The need for toleration would not arise if there were not disapproval. Perhaps 'respect for others' can be seen as a procedural value as well as a moral virtue; but then the case is no better: total respect is either lack of moral discrimination or is love (and love in any absolute sense is plainly an unrealistic and unnecessary precondition for civil society). Toleration is a two-dimensional concept: both disapproval but also restraint, forbearance and hopefully respect are signalled – hopefully mutual respect. Thus to be tolerant is to express or imply a disapproval, but in a fair way and without forcing it on another. But absence of force does not at all imply absence of any attempt to persuade or refusal to signal some degree of disapproval. What is fair and just by way of persuasion will be relative to the circumstance. (We surely, to make a small point in passing, expect to be exposed to different sorts of influence and information in the classroom than in adult committee

157

meetings.) It is important for citizenship learning to grasp the difference between toleration and permissiveness – an often futile debate. 'Permissiveness' may, indeed, imply not caring whether something is done or not, or else a full acceptance of a person or a pattern of social behaviour. But from the fact of a person caring, it does not logically follow that the person must be in favour of legal restraints: he or she may be in favour of toleration, for instance of allowing the behaviour but making disapproval clear, and of toleration up to a point.

To give what is to some a difficult instance. I am a humanist, but I respect the sincerity of religious belief – including Islam. I am tolerant of most Islamic practices. But of marriage without consent, I note gladly that British law is not tolerant. I have no difficulty with that position whatever. Certainly toleration should not be encouraged as an end in itself; it is simply a response to living together amid conflicts of values. Therefore it is, I suggest, a procedural value; and it can be learnt at a very early age in classroom discussions, even or especially in primary school 'circle time'. Neutrality is not to be encouraged: to be biased is human and to attempt to unbias people is to emasculate or silence them. Bias as such is not to be condemned out of hand, only to condemn that gross bias which leads to false perceptions of the nature of other interests, groups and ideas. Teachers, educational institutions and political regimes are not to be condemned for bias or for anything as natural and inevitable as attempting to maintain themselves and their identities; they are only, in terms of reason, human rights and education, to be condemned if they do so in an intolerant manner and in such a way as to repress deliberately or to suppress unpleasant facts, contrary opinions, rival doctrines, challenging theories.

Two important inferences can be drawn from the concept: firstly, that someone who is politically literate will hold views of their own, but will hold them in such a way as to be tolerant of the views of others; and secondly, that as tolerance in part depends on knowledge of the behaviour and beliefs associated with other viewpoints, this knowledge should be taught and pupils should be tested in their powers of empathy. 'How would a Conservative, a Lib-Dem or a Labour supporter react to this [stated] problem and what justifications would they give?' And 'play the role of Scottish or a Welsh Nationalist in this [stated] situation.' These are all (once) familiar devices which help strengthen an important component of political literacy. A lot of RE is taught this way.

Empathy is a skill to be developed quite as much as self-expression and the propensity to participate, indeed it strengthens both. Toleration is neither simply a disposition towards nor knowledge of others, but is both together. Even in political life, empathy has great tactical value. The dogmatic activist all too often fails to understand his opponents, commonly hanging them all together as 'Fascists' or 'Marxists', and therefore adopts inappropriate tactics. 'Know thy enemy as thyself', said Koestler to Orwell.

Fairness

'Fairness' may seem vague compared to 'justice', but it is the concept of common usage. Also John Rawls, in the most ambitious modern attempt to state a philosophical theory of justice, resolves the overly legalistic, traditional discussions of justice into the more general considerations of what is thought to be fair and what is fair (Rawls, 1972). Earlier, though certainly influenced by Rawls, W. G. Runciman's work on equality and the concept of 'relative deprivation' showed empirically that working people judged other peoples' wages not in absolute monetary terms but by whether the differences were 'fair' or not (some were thought to be fair, some not) (Runciman, 1966). He concluded like Rawls that whereas equality cannot be stated precisely as a social goal or justified in general terms as an ideal, 'less unjustifiable inequalities' (or less unfairness) can. So it is reasonable to demand that all inequalities should justify themselves. (And it is right and fair, he adds, to *respect* all men equally, but unfair to *praise* them equally.)

Certainly fairness, however vague, is to be preferred to the misleading precision of 'rule of law' which many would make a prerequisite both for political-democratic order and for citizenship education. 'What rules of law?' can be asked. If only there were, but that begs the question. Must we adhere to rules in general so long as they have been legitimately made or derived whatever their context or outcome? Perhaps, but then *have they* been fairly made or derived? That may be the educational question to ask; otherwise making 'rule of law' a basic value begs the question and usually smuggles into an argument about procedural rules some highly substantive (and usually highly traditional) content. Anyway, 'are the rules fair?' is a prior question to 'is it fair by the rules?' You must convince me that it is fair. A propensity to obey rules in general is surely good if the rules are good. Plato, after all (and no democrat he), long ago distinguished between law and justice. Socrates was a good man – who broke the law; so did Jesus. We cannot hide behind such a vague formula as 'rule of law'; we have got to come out, in the classroom as well as (hopefully) our leaders in the media, and justify every instance that is challenged, defend it or abandon it, not claim that they all hang together because they are the law; and that bad decisions must be forgiven because of all the accumulation of good decisions (which is often what public authorities mean by the 'rule of law'). Besides, it simply is not true that we need to know what the rules are before we can effectively and responsibly participate in politics or, for instance, play football. Football, even played reasonably fairly, long preceded the existence of known or enforceable rules; and a precise knowledge of them would not be high in the list of relevant skills for a professional's advancement. Certainly, as I never tire of saying, knowledge of constitutional rules, real or imagined, is a very poor beginning for a genuine political education. In countries with written constitutions we find that some citizenship education, far from seeking to encourage active citizenship, too often takes refuge in the safe haven of learning the articles of the constitutions, federal and state.

160

The simplest statement of Rawls on 'fairness' would be that we should accept an outcome as fair if we can imagine that we were party, along with all others likely to be affected, in a state of equality (or equality of influence) to establishing rules to settle disputes without prior knowledge of the outcome. He might have used the example of those primary schools where young pupils are encouraged to make their own rules. In other words, 'fairness' follows from what in principle we would accept as a proper way of making decisions without knowing whether the outcome of the process will benefit or harm us. All this sounds very abstract. But the politically literate person will question whether the distribution of goods, rewards and praise is fair or not. And he or she will be satisfied (or not) that it is fair by being asked and asking the further question, 'Can you think of a better way of doing it that would be acceptable to others?'

The attacker is tripped in the penalty area in the last minute, penalty given and the decisive goal scored. Four reactions may follow from the losers. (i) 'Not fair to lose by a penalty', which is both invalid as an argument and unethical; (ii) 'That's the rule, what the Ref says it is', which implies a passive fear of the referee or an Hobbesean assumption that one may break a rule if not caught; or (iii) a calm or even grudging 'Fair enough' – which is fair enough and the best we usually hope for. But if (iv) the defender improbably said, with happy civic virtue and self-righteousness, 'Well I declare, that's a good example of what happens if we break the rules; we deserved that' we *might* judge this man to be politically illiterate even if, of course, 'well-taught'.

Respect for truth

Here it will be immediately objected that, even in a parliamentary democracy, the practice of politics and citizenship education do not always see eye to eye. But I mean something more basic than that: politicians are not the only, indeed are not the main, source of political knowledge. If one lives in a society where relevant truths cannot be told publicly about how government is conducted or what politics is about, then political education is impossible. Anything that is even potentially relevant to how government is conducted, how decisions are made, how the individuals may perceive what their interests are and how they may defend them, anything such must be capable of being stated publicly; and if believed to be true, some evidence must be stateable at any level of education in which the questions can arise, however simplified it has to be. If the full truth is too difficult to grasp, or is simply unknown, then conventional fictions (which may strictly speaking be, at worst, lies, or at best evasions) should never be put forward, either for mistaken social or moral reasons or simply to have simpler models – i.e. the stork, the Queen as ruler, the British constitution, the Prime Minister as above the battle, the Cabinet as collective and dispassionate wisdom, the House of Commons as 659 individual members elected for and by constituents in the general interest (with no thought of Party), civil servants never involved in making policy, or that there is 'no such thing as Society', or as 'class' for that matter, or that each social class has a clear mind of its own, etc., etc. Simplification must not involve falsification, however innocent the motives. When the teller of white lies is found out, it is he or she who has discredited legitimate authority not the critic.

A politically literate person will ask awkward questions early. Political literacy must involve knowing that truths have to be faced, however embarrassing or difficult. The child is surely shocked by parents quarrelling openly with hysterical selfishness. If Joe and Joanne have to be made aware why this can happen in the world, this does not imply habituating them to it. Individuals can only grow and societies improve amid the tension between knowing what the facts are and wishing to change or modify them.

Formidable arguments based upon 'reasons of state' were once made that there are some things only knowable by natural rulers and that there is some knowledge that must always be kept from the people if order is to be preserved – the

162

arcana imperii or the mysteries of power. This might seem utterly discredited. But some modern concepts of ideology are sophisticated versions of this old *politique* argument: that those who really understand the ideology, the inner party, or the freelance dialecticians, know that it is best for everyone if propaganda and indoctrination could replace the elitist, humanist practice of genuine critical education — for the moment, of course, until conditions are right for freedom and truth-speaking and no censorship. Truth is what is useful to the cause. The 'ideologically correct' is what the truth will be tomorrow (if we can get our hands on you today), rather than what you miserable, supine load of brainwashed brothers and sisters, if you talk quietly among yourselves, happen to think it is right now. But as modern writers like Orwell and Koestler have argued, there is a simple sense in which a lie is still a lie, and a half-truth is a half-lie, whether told for country or party; and that regimes that depend upon systematic lies are neither worthy of support, nor likely to be stable without systematic coercive oppression. But if these opponents cannot make enough capital out of exposing the untruths of autocracy but invent their own counter-myths and ideologies, then this is a sure sign that they are trying to make too much capital too fast and before the shareholders wake up to see what is happening. There is, of course, a more common and mundane parliamentary version of this: that only those who 'really understand' how the government machine works can say what it is in the public interest to put before the public.

Put positively, one necessary condition of a free and just regime is that the truth can be discovered and publicly told about how all decisions of government are made. There are obvious practical limitations: security, anticipation of economic decisions, confidentiality and libel. There are occasions, in times of emergency, in which limitations on truth-telling and public expression are justifiable. But the literate person must presume a right to know and that everything should be told unless there are compelling and generally acceptable known reasons to the contrary. If there are occasions when for the safety of the state truth should not be told, in political education these must be presented as extraordinarily exceptional, as calling for very special justifications and reasons. In hard times lying or just not telling the truth can be regarded as a test of party loyalty or even patriotism, but never of a political education. Particular governments may be damaged, but it is a test of free regimes that no amount of truth-telling can endanger them.

Respect for reasoning

It may be otiose to include respect for reasoning as a precondition for citizenship education. But it may need stressing that to be politically literate means a willingness to give reasons (however ill-formed or simple) why one holds a view and to give justifications for one's actions, and to demand them of others. For some have held, a still powerful cultural tendency and educational doctrine, that if an opinion is *sincerely* held, it should not be questioned (a belief that all prejudices are equal), nor should justifications be pressed for in respect of actions that are held to be *authentic* expressions of personality (going with an amiable belief that no feelings should be hurt by being questioned rigorously). Others regard reasons as unnecessary if actions can be certified as authentic or typical emanations of some group interest – 'working-class solidarity', 'middle-class moderation' or 'my ethnic community', for instance. Some progressives, after having properly attacked Burkean ideas that prejudices drawn from experience and tradition are a sufficient guide to political conduct, have now made a cult of sincerity, authenticity or typicality. Sincerity, authenticity, spontaneity, typicality, etc., are values to be cultivated, but not as a cult or a one-crop moral economy; such values must grow alongside others. Since politics is so much concerned with consequences on others, it is of fundamental importance that reasons shall always be given and justifications offered for effects unwelcome to some others.

Another reason why this great part of our Western political tradition that came from the Greeks is not to be taken for granted, that politics involves reasoning among fellow citizens, is because too often such political education as there is comes not from schools but from the example of press campaigns and how leading political figures wage election campaigns. A young person can easily form the opinion that politics is (i) a residual claim to govern on the simple ground that the other side is inherently stupid and tells so many lies; (ii) simply the expression of social interests; and (iii) simply an auction of speculative benefits for probable support. So little reasoning and canvassing of principles enters into current electoral campaigning that politics may seem just a question of 'who gets what, when and how'.

Respect for reasoning comes from analogy and examples in the polity, the home and the school. We are only discussing the latter, but the context is always there. The teacher must give reasons why things are done in certain ways, particularly when meeting a new class or when changes are made. It is beside the point to object that reasons given to young children may often not be understood; for the real point is that the habit of giving reasons and expecting them to be given is basic both to intellectual method (as distinct from memorizing) and to political democracy (as distinct from passive obedience). I do not understand why I should do some of the things the doctor tells me to do, but I do believe (usually rightly) that he could explain if I asked (and I get worried if he refuses even to try). Of course there is much more to it than this, for I know that there are other doctors (mostly of the older generation, happily) who see any questions as questioning their authority. Part of political literacy is knowing that there are both alternative means towards any end and alternative sources of information.

The giving of reasons, even the obligation to give reasons and to justify what one teaches and how, does not destroy legitimate authority – on the contrary, the refusal to give reasons encourages either passivity or rebellion. The indulgent

165

permissive view that all reasons are equally subjective ('post-modern', is it?), simply enshrines sincerity, self-expression and authenticity as king, as against reason, truth and compassion; so that then all authority is seen as bad authority. A basic part of political literacy is to be able to distinguish between power and authority. Few types of authority can subsist on coercion alone, but then some authority is justifiable and some not. In general political philosophers have seen authority as justifiable when it fulfils expertly or skilfully some function widely agreed to be needed. To exercise authority is not, as such, to be authoritarian: to be authoritarian is when 'an authority' seeks to exercise power beyond the admitted function. The simplest form of authoritarianism is the extension of legitimate authority into topics and areas in which it has no relevance and competence. Education, both in home and school, can be seen as a process of increasing differentiation of function; thus the authority of both the parent and the school are originally very wide and generalized, but then they need to become more and more specific as children grow older. Within the accepted areas, the authority can actually be stronger. But such authority depends on giving reasons thought relevant by those affected.

Similarly it is not intolerant as such to disapprove of people's viewpoints and to express the disapproval, only if the disapproval (by 'authority', for instance) refuses to hear contradictions and suppresses opportunities for dissent. 'Taking advantage of one's position' is not wrong, indeed is usually proper, and often a duty – if, and only if, 'the others are given a fair chance'. Obviously a respect for reasoning and for legitimate (that is specified) authority is part of all education, not specifically political education. The question how much political attitudes are conditioned by the general organization of the school as distinct from particular teaching within the school is, I would suggest, an empirical question – on which little reliable research has been done. But we are not impressed by the *a priori* argument that reforms of school organization, still less 'ethos', are the only way to get a better political education. The argument that the school is a good model of the general political system, to be studied as such, must seem of limited truth even in the United States where it is often heard; here it seems faintly ridiculous (unless – the clearest cases – some are taken as models of benign autocracy). But *a priori* we might suspect that important negative relations exist: the kind of presuppositions to political literacy that we are discussing could hardly be expected to flourish in those few schools, for instance, where children can still see a head teacher interrupt his colleagues without apology or warning, and know that nothing is ever discussed between those 'authorities' whom they know and respect, their teachers, and 'the authority', the one person of power, the head.

* * *

My original audience may have been disappointed by my not talking directly about the work of the Citizenship Report of 1998, but rather in trying to consider what I thought the presuppositions of such an activity to be. These might amaze most of the members of the committee – highly practical men and women. But practice – as Oakshott argued (and I suppose I am a kind of left-wing Oakshottian) – is always an abridgement of experience, an experience that is both a tradition of practice and an intellectual tradition, or our way of perceiving and understanding a particular history in a changing context. Those who think themselves to be purely practical are always deceiving or underestimating themselves. We all need some help and some needling to understand our own presuppositions.

10 The d█████ █████ ██l thinking in Br█████ ██████ ████

█████ █████ ██████ n *Critical Review of International* ████ ████ ████ *sophy*, **1** (1, Spring 1998). (I am ████ ██ ████ & Co and to the editor, Professor █████ ████ ██ mission to reprint it.) Written at the █████ ████ █e advisory group on Citizenship and █████ ██ ████ ools was deliberating, it shows that I feel █████ █████ olitical literacy' is not only lacking among █████ ████ ol leavers, but also among many of those w█ █████ ontrol their standards – a view that could only be tac█ ly hinted at in the Advisory Group's Report of 1998 (see para. 1.9(b)).

Thirty years ago political philosophy in Britain was feared to be dead or dying, dying of meaninglessness and neglect. So all the sages said. Political philosophy now enjoys a golden age, certainly in the English-speaking world; but never has the level of political debate been lower. The memories are still painful of how, in the American presidential campaign of 1996 and the British general election of 1997, even sustained rhetoric, let alone attempts at reasoned, persuasive discourse, finally collapsed into soundbites, and contingent soundbites at that, mainly reacting to relatively trivial, mainly opportunistic accusations and counter-accusations, a plethora of soundbites rarely exhibiting either Bagehot's 'stream of tendency' or a coherent 'moral discourse'. All three main parties talked about restoring a sense of morality to politics, but found some difficulty in spelling out what they meant, or even spelling it at all. Never more political knowledge, either, with the growth of political science; but never less use made of it in public life, unless psephology is the name of the game.

The paradox vanishes if I had written '*academic* political philosophy enjoys a golden age' and 'the level of *public* political debate' has never been lower. There is so much up there in the ivory tower but so little seeps down. Most of the time we are (or were) talking to our own students. This is in a remarkable contrast to a hundred years ago and even earlier when 'public' could still be attached to 'political philosophy'. A recent essayist (Garnett, 1993) lamented 'the decline of the theoretical polemic' compared to the early nineteenth century, a time when if there was no political thought coming out of the ancient universities, even if some Benthamism in the new London University, yet there were the *Edinburgh* and the *Westminster* reviews commanding the talent of public intellectuals, publicists, thinkers, call them what you will; and the Mills, Macaulay, Sidney Smith, Brougham, Hazlitt and others were well answered in well-grounded kind by the *Quarterly*'s Tory team of Lockhart, Croker, Southey and Walter Scott among others. Today one could conjure up a list of prominent public intellectuals, perhaps running intellectual chat shows; but rarely are they political intellectuals; and what they say in passing about politics is at best commonplace, too often cynical. The point hardly needs labouring.

Around the turn of the century the discourse of the 'New Liberals' and of the new Socialists somehow had an impact on the discourse of leading politicians, some of whom were political thinkers, perhaps not always in terms to satisfy a modern seminar in political philosophy, but certainly thoughtful about politics, and accustomed to setting out reasoned grounds for their conclusions (Freeden, 1978). These Liberals often gave the impression of reasoning themselves into unlikely conclusions. Unlike so many leaders of our times, however, they were not, in Hannah Arendt's terms, 'thoughtless'. Modern political rhetoric has become not merely banal but also routinized. The point is *not* to say anything different.

170

But there was in the 1900s a considerable class of men (it was, of course, almost all men – in that world, at once so near and so distant, Beatrice Webbs were few and far between), some of whom were in the universities, some in Parliament, mostly in the professions, some landowning gentlemen with intellectual tastes or persuasions, who read what each other wrote, usually knew each other, or knew of each other quite well, and were accustomed to give, whether in books, articles or letters to *The Times* and the then many elsewheres for that kind of level of public debate, dailies, weeklies and monthlies, *reasons for what they said*. Today all that is asked of their heirs is simply to state opinions with as much appearance of sincerity as appears natural on the box. Those men were 'the public moralists' of Stefan Collini's subtle and illuminating study of 'political thought and intellectual life in Britain, 1850–1930' (Collini, 1991). There was, in other words, what Walter Lippmann had called 'a public philosophy' – already feeling in the 1930s that it was in danger of being drowned in a democratic flood of mere opinion, and indeed deified by being studied scientifically as he had pioneered in his youth (Lippmann, 1914 and 1954).

These men were an elite, predominantly but not exclusively a specifically Liberal elite, as well as liberal-minded (but there was Fitz-James Stephens as well as Leslie Stephens), in socialist eyes not so much a counter-establishment as part of the establishment; but none the less, they were a highly literate elite who wrote in an intellectually demanding but, to any who cared to make the effort, a completely accessible manner. Collini does not discuss the socialist movement, even if there is a case that J. S. Mill was father of them all (as is more clear to modern Tory historians – say Maurice Cowling – than it was to James Bryce, A. V. Dicey, W. E. H. Lecky and John Morley, for example). But it is clear that the Socialist tracts of William Morris found a keen and literate audience among working men and women as well as middle-class intellectuals, as did the tracts, speeches and myriad newspaper articles of George Bernard Shaw, even if not his plays. The evidence is clear that the Victorian newly literate would tackle books and tracts of a subject matter and complexity far beyond the interests, if not the formal ability of the formally better educated, certainly far longer educated, working and lower middle classes of today. The most common first book, and the book most commonly purchased, possessed and even read, was, after all, a book of astounding complexity and rich but difficult language, the Bible. To its new possessors the new literacy, the product of compulsory secondary education and the free public library movement, was a wonder and a weapon to be used to the hilt, before the Yellow Press began, slowly but surely, to exploit and debase its possibilities, long before one could put the newspaper down, or not even pick one up, to relax in front of the TV. If one reads Orwell's *Nineteen Eighty-Four* as savage Swiftian satire not as prophecy, then one notices that the proles, unlike the inner party, are controlled by debasement more than direct terror: they are given what we think they want, controlling their choices, not propaganda but 'prole-feed' through 'newspapers containing almost nothing except sport, crime, and astrology, sensational five-cent novelettes, films oozing with sex, and sentimental songs which were composed entirely by mechanical means on a special kind of kaleidoscope known as a versificator' (Orwell, 1949). The culture of competitive capitalism works like God in mysterious ways its wonders of social control to perform. Perhaps this reminds one that we should look for serious political thinking in imaginative literature as well as in the academy or the press (Whitebrook, 1992 and 1995).

It would be covering familiar ground to contrast, say, the standard of debate on the Irish Question in the 1880s with that of today, the running debate from the 1870s to the 1930s on the extent and nature of imperialism with that on Britain's relations with the EC today, or the debates on constitutional reform and 'home rule all round' before 1914 with the similar debate now – that is if one is talking of a discourse beyond the academy. Whether one looks at books, journals, press articles or parliamentary debates, the comparison is not comfortable to ourselves. I find it worrying, especially when there has been no underpinning of citizenship education in schools and colleges. One must look away from political writing to imaginative literature, philosophy, historical studies and biography to see any sign of what that earlier generation would have called 'mental progress'.

The retreat of academia

The academy, however, has never been better. There is a plethora of books and articles of great learning and thoughtfulness on these constitutional questions. Political thinking and constitutional law are coming together under our eyes, and jurisprudence is being reborn or, rather, reconstituted not as positivism in the Austinian manner but as something moral, pluralistic and political, as Herbert Hart and Neil MacCormick pointed towards. But there are few signs that this academic thinking reaches even what publishers call 'the intelligent reading public', let alone that they reach any reading politicians, except occasionally in the ephemeral form of a thousand-word article in the broadsheets. Most MPs now have a university degree, but if they are intellectual at all, they are so in the mode of newsprint, broadcasting and increasingly IT, the Web and the Net, rarely through book or tract. True, there was recently an active Fabian political philosophy group of academics and, for a brief while, some academics and intellectuals strove to give content to the rhetoric or aspiration of New Labour's Third Way.

Most academics, however, feel no frustration in pursuing purely professional careers, albeit a peculiar profession without obvious clients or beneficiaries except the transitory students; and one in which professional esteem and career advancement comes solely from writing for each other, rarely if ever from attempting to relate either to the polity or to educational issues affecting the whole population. This may, indeed, be part of a proper definition of scholarship, even if an incomplete one; but there is something paradoxical about

173

politics as a discipline so rarely relating to politics as an activity. Researchers and thinkers in think-tanks imagine themselves to be mediators between specialized knowledge and the public mind, but if their morale depended on knowing that their messages were heard, rather than on having an agreeable intellectual job, it could be very low, and sometimes is. Perhaps the new generation of reforming MPs, having university degrees already, many or most in the social sciences of some form or other, think they know it already: outside advice, or even knowledge to be used without the advice, is not needed. The academy is Count Frankenstein and they are our monster children, doing, of course, like our own real children, 'me own thing'. The tradition of political thinking now sustains the Cambridge University Press but not even the *Guardian*, the *Independent*, the *Observer* or the *New Statesman*. *The Times*, the *Daily Telegraph* and the *Spectator* mock thinkers all, the higher philistinism.

Political philosophy has become in all its modes, whether historical, analytical or moral, an academic discipline of the highest scholarly standards, both in publications and in intellectual debate. But it has become almost entirely internalized. We talk to ourselves loudly and brilliantly. When celebrated breakouts are made, as if political philosophers might have something to say to politicians and those who act like citizens (a pity the word 'activist' is tarnished), then even the style, mental vigour and fame of an Isaiah Berlin would not reach beyond a modern intellectual community who are far less politically involved or, to use the old phrase, far less 'public-spirited', than in the early years of the century. The views of John Rawls on equality in his magisterial *A Theory of Justice* (Rawls, 1972) were, however, once taken up by Bryan Gould, albeit with some reservations, in a book written while a front-bench Labour spokesman (Gould, 1985). Gould still saw equality as a substantive goal, if always on a receding horizon, and did not accept that Rawls's procedural principle would have a great egalitarian cutting edge if ever seriously applied: that all inequalities of reward must be justified by showing that they add to the general good. But now Tony Blair in his writings and speeches only espouses 'equality of opportunity', indeed speaks warmly of wanting a 'meritocracy', as if Michael Young had never analysed and satirized its dangers and disadvantages (perhaps one of the last of Collini's Edwardian public moralists) (Young, 1958). Professionalization now seems to have become an end in itself. Some thinking and writing must always be for the concerns of a profession; but there is something at once tragic and comic in a profession of political studies that has so little contact with the activities of politics (Ricci, 1984).

I do not argue for commitment. That is too easy an answer, and often there has been too much of that. Preaching revolutionary politics in the 1970s and 1980s in a discourse unintelligible even to most educated people, let alone 'the People', carried few risks within university walls, and none whatever without. I argue for relevance and an independent-minded critical engagement, not commitment or unquestioning loyalty to a party. If something we are studying is relevant to civic life, then some pains should be taken to write up the research in a form that is accessible to intelligent citizens, or at least capable of being plagiarized by the small and diminishing number of columnists, editorial writers and radio or TV producers who do still read demanding books. Outside the walls of academia, economists are held in high regard. Even if their policy recommendations or projections occasionally prove wrong, it is commonly believed that their analytical techniques can narrow the range of alternatives and comment usefully on the probable consequences of alternative policies. Few people now believe that the analytical methods of academic political philosophers should have any relevance to the political thinking of ordinary citizens. But two examples of commonly used and abused concepts might suggest the contrary. Consider the popular confusion, and the emotions aroused, over 'federalism' and 'sovereignty' – terms which the most surprising people, who would scorn theory and extol unappraised practice, throw about freely.

175

Essays on citizenship

Federalism and sovereignty: an example

We have been threatened with or occasionally promised *a federal superstate* and have been told that if we 'lose our sovereignty' then we 'lose our identity'. Now 'superstate' must surely mean a very strong state, usually in the modern world a highly centralized state, and sometimes even, but not always, a sovereign state. But a federal state is one where states have come together to create in a legal framework a negotiated distribution of power. The centre may be relatively strong, or relatively weak, but if it is federal, then it is negotiated and cannot be a superstate. Those who use the phrase are either very confused or demagogic and rhetorical. (Whether the rhetoric is effective or not is, of course, another question.)

Many people must get confused when they hear famous advocates of a strong central state (needed to stop local authorities spending money and pursuing different social policies from the government) talk of a 'federal superstate'. How is the adjective federal meant to strengthen the neutral term state into something threatening? For a federal structure surely implies, however we define it, a system of negotiated and then legalized restraints on a central state.

This has seemed so obvious to Americans, Canadians, Australians, etc. that they rarely speak of 'the state', but rather of 'the federal government and the states'. They appear able to live without any great 'sense of the state', indeed when governments claim to be sovereign, John Adams, one of the Founding Fathers, famously said 'sovereignty is very tyranny'. They saw a direct contradiction between a federal order with a constitution that bound even the government and doctrine of sovereignty, even the English doctrine of the sovereignty of Parliament (for all autocrats were claiming to be sovereign). When the American colonists claimed that Parliament had no sovereign right to tax them (as Tony Blair on the campaign trail quite correctly reminded Scotland that the Westminster Parliament will still be sovereign when there is a Scottish parliament), Lord North famously asserted the

176

absolute right to tax. He argued from what was for him both a self-evident proposition of natural order (the Great Chain of Being indeed) and the essence of the British constitution as clearly stated in the Declaratory Act of 1766. But Edmund Burke, while conceding both the right to tax and that there was and had to be an absolute sovereign power residing, as Blackstone had said, in Parliament, yet argued in his great speech 'On Conciliation with America' that sovereign power must always be exercised with prudence: 'The question with me is not whether you have a right to render your people miserable; but whether it is not your interest to make them happy. It is not what a lawyer tells me I may do; but what humanity, reason and justice tells I ought to do.'

Those are the only terms in which sovereignty can work. The misanthrope of Malmesbury knew this well. Leviathan's power collapses if it threatens the lives, possibly even the property of its subjects. The Westminster Parliament became sovereign under the Act of Union of 1707, indeed; but Scotland was largely left to govern itself through local magnates (the famous 'Dundas despotism') and maintained all its national institutions except the Parliament (which was, in our terms, no more representative or democratic than that of England – possibly less, if that now matters; and in any case it was at the time a far less important symbol of the national identity than the Presbyterian Church, established as a consequence of the Treaty of Union). The old English Tories, with their personal territorial possessions and some sense of history, knew that the retention of sovereignty depended, except in times of national emergency, more on the restraint of power than its exercise. Irish and Scottish nationalist history once painted a picture of oppression; true, on decisive occasions, but mainly the old Tories played a kind of cultural politics and had an easy, somewhat cynical, somewhat romantic, tolerance of indigenous cultures and institutions. India began to be governed in that way too: not 'divide and rule', but ruling through existing divisions and, as far as possible, existing laws and customs. The suburban Europhobe New Conservatives do not

177

know this: to them, if you have power, you use it (whether to party or personal advantage). To summarize social history lucidly if a little briefly, they are no longer gentlemen (Crick, 1995).

The old Tories had a sense of the diversity of nations in the United Kingdom, each calling for different adjustments. Failure in Ireland, certainly but success in keeping Scotland and Wales in the union (note the word 'union' is not 'state'). The New Conservatives have little sense of actual history, but only of what Neal Ascherson has well called 'the blue mist of heritage'; so by blundering misgovernment they stirred national feeling in Scotland into taking a political form; and on the Europe question they have totally confused sovereignty with power, thus confusing themselves and others, and actually diminishing British power – if by power one means influence over others and the ability to carry out premeditated intentions, not simply to be unchallenged on a paper throne.

Mr Enoch Powell was wont to tell us the precise day we lost our sovereignty, as if it was virginity in a nunnery – what the Oxford philosopher Gilbert Ryle used to call 'a category mistake', like 'I have seen the colleges, but where is the university?' But if we had retained our sovereignty, then we would have been, if not powerless, at least far less able to promote the economic interests of our country. We restrained, or some say shared, our sovereignty for clear and sensible economic and also political reasons (a concert of European nations who could never go to war with themselves again). The British Eurosceptics say they wish to maintain a free-trade area and are not anti-European (some are, some aren't). But it is a very strange idea of a market that does not recognize its dependence on both legal rules and moral restraints regarding fair competition (they should actually read Adam Smith), and the fewer moral restraints there are the more the need for legal restraints. A clear contradiction exists in the New Conservatism between market philosophy and nationalism, philosophically pulling them into absurdities like 'federal superstate' and psychologically into xenophobia and paranoia (*they* will do us down, take away our identity, our Queen, our money, etc.), as if all would be well for us were we but all alone in the world. I truly believe that the practice or tradition of clear political thinking can at least diminish or contain xenophobia and paranoia. Philosophical contradictions with practical implications can hardly help prudent political calculation.

Thinking about identity

The reasons for the displacement of the old Tory skills of political prudence by ultra-nationalism are fairly obvious, contingent rather than ideological; but the contingencies have favoured some parts of the ideology more than others. Psychologically they have never got used to accepting the post-war diminishment of British power, which is sad enough, and seem to think that history is reversible, so 'make Britain great again' – which unfortunately is not mere rhetoric for them, and their rhetoric can grow on others. It is a rhetoric of bitter nostalgia not of tolerant and realistic modernization. 'We will lose our identity if we go further in!' This raises large questions, about which political philosophers may not agree but which they can at least clarify, or at the very least see that 'state', 'sovereignty', 'power', 'nation' and 'identity' carry different meanings, are not to be conflated in a rhetoric of a combined 'threat to all those things we hold most dear'. Personally I hold my common sense dear, so I ask that even if we were to imagine with Euro-sceptic angst a European superstate by the middle of the twenty-first century, would the Dutch still not be Dutch, the French French, the Germans Germans, the Greeks Greeks indeed, etc. etc.? Culture seems stronger than political institutions.

Look under our noses. Living in Scotland I often heard a mistaken rhetoric: that 'we Scots will lose our identity if we do not have a parliament'. But nearly three centuries of history contradict this loaded fear. Scottishness is still very alive, and kicking and ever changing – the Scotland of James Kellman, Billy Connolly and Donald Dewar is not that of either Robert

Burns or Walter Scott (Nairn, 1988). The case for a Scottish parliament is a democratic case, not one based on a threat to identity or the mistaken view that there cannot be a nation without a sovereign state (Patterson, 1994).

But there is a problem, a problem for the English precisely because the United Kingdom is a multinational state in which people have dual identities – Scottish and British, Welsh and British, yes, Irish and British even, Asian and British, etc. This has been historically possible because the old English governing class understood the diversity and did not develop, as almost everywhere else, a state cult English nationalism. It would have been unhelpful to the main business of British government: holding the United Kingdom together. The political thinkers or 'public moralists' described by Collini were well aware of the distinctions between a sovereign state and a federal state and they were careful to push Britishness, not an all-embracing Englishness; certainly they were aware of a distinction and of how politically important it was to observe it. The test of this is found in the subject catalogue of any major library. Shelves full of books are to be found on Irish, Scottish and Welsh nationalism, but only a handful on English nationalism. Before the Second World War two concepts of loyalty and legitimation filled the emotional gap for the English of this lack of explicitness: the Crown and the Empire. Both were open to the four nations, even to Kipling's 'lesser breeds within the law'. Now that the Empire has gone and the Crown has discredited and minimalized itself, perhaps we need more not less English nationalism, a way of looking at English identity that respects and parallels those senses of Scottish and Welsh identity which readily coexist, when the centre is prudent and sensitive, with a Britishness. They can do so when 'Britishness' is not seen as an entire culture, but simply as the common institutions of Parliament, Crown and law within which Scottish, Welsh and English identities live their own, if always interrelated, lives. The new immigrants see this more clearly than the Europhobes. They want to live their own lives within the protection of British laws, not to become English; they wish to respect those laws and to be respected, not as if English but as, for example 'British and Asian' (one rarely if ever hears 'English and Asian') (Modood, 1992). It is the English who compound and confuse Britishness with Englishness.

Perhaps if there had been more serious, critical but respectful, discussion of Englishness on the Left (not all that too easy mocking and cynicism of the satire shows, et cetera), there would be less paranoia on the Right in the debate about the future of our established and necessary relations with the EC. Modern English intellectuals have no difficulty trying to characterize differences between modern English, Scottish, Irish, Welsh and American novels and poetry, but fail to do this seriously, only satirically and dismissively, of English politics. It was an old, sad failing of the English Left to defend almost everyone else's nationalism as, however violent and ethnocentric, at least 'authentic' whereas their own was artificial, nothing but false consciousness. Orwell was the great exception to this (Orwell, 1941). But it is not nationalism that is wrong, but only a nationalism that claims to exclude other real identities in each of us, or that is backward looking, tied to an historically contingent idea of sovereignty. Sovereignty is not a universal part of the human condition. It had a beginning in the sixteenth century as a theory of how government should be conducted, and is likely to have an end in the twenty-first century when, indeed, federal forms are more likely in most parts of the world to express interdependence. The public ethic of such states will stress mutual dependence and mutual respect, but will by no means possible or desirable abolish national identities. We may actually be able to take more pride and pleasure in national differences once they appear less threatening. 'All power', said Harold Laski, 'is federal' (Laski, 1925). But who today outside the academy would think of reading Laski's books, even though, after his first two books on the theory and history of the concept of sovereignty, everything he wrote was meant to be accessible to the serious general reader (although that admirable intention does not automatically earn a seal of quality). And publishers were happy. There was, after all, at that time in Britain only a small university market.

Decline of the political book

Walter Bagehot once sententiously remarked that the reason there were so few good political books was that few people who can write well know anything. And nowadays, with the growth of the social sciences, many more people know a lot but cannot write – certainly not in a way that is publicly accessible. And the 1997 general election has revealed a new type of political writer who does know a lot, who can write, or else Penguin would not have commissioned them for what proved to be three widely abused *Why I Vote For ...* books, but who were each under obvious and awful constraint to say as little as possible that might even appear to be outside the party line; and what was worse, the restraint was almost certainly self-imposed (Wallace, 1997; Willetts, 1997; Wright, 1997). One doubts if Peter Mandelson, Brian Mawhinney or Paddy Ashdown had time to read proofs in the immediate pre-election period.

In the 1930s good political books were common, today they are few. (If that sounds a wee bit categorical or *ipse dixit* it comes from ten years as literary editor of *The Political Quarterly* and six as a judge for the Orwell prize for political writing.) But if the proof of the pudding has to be in the eating, then consider Penguin's list of books in print. They used to be the leading non-academic political publisher. Currently there are two and three-quarter columns of books listed under 'Politics' (the majority of them primarily for the university market) and 19 columns under 'New Age', nearly all written to be accessible to the general reader! Now Swampie is king, for a day.

'What I have most wanted to do', Orwell famously wrote, 'is to make political writing into an art.' He wanted to bring intellectuals into politics not simply by nagging them that freedom depends on good politics, but by reassuring them that artistic integrity need not be the price of commitment. When he wrote 'No writer can be a loyal member of a political party', the stress must have been on 'loyal'. For at that time he was a member of a political party. In 1941 in *Horizon* he bit hard a big hand that had fed him. In an essay titled 'Wells, Hitler and the World State' he railed that H. G. Wells had underestimated Hitler, making him a figure of fun, not realizing his deadly seriousness; and spouting 'world government now!' as an impractical answer to immediate crises, idealism not as goal but as an escape from reality. Orwell saw Wells as reflecting, like too many intellectuals, indeed he threw the whole of 'the Left Book Club' into the charge sheet for fair measure, 'the sheltered conditions of English life'. But 'in Europe' something different stirred:

> One development of the last ten years has been the appearance of the 'political book', a sort of enlarged pamphlet combining history with political criticism, as an important literary form. But the best writers in this line – Trotsky, Rauschning, Rosenberg, Silone, Borkenau, Koestler and others – have none of them been Englishmen, and nearly all of them have been renegades from one or other extremist party, who have seen totalitarianism at close quarters and know the meaning of exile and persecution.
>
> (Orwell, 1994)

If the polemic at Wells seems fair enough, his sideswipes at his fellow English either implied unrealistically high standards for political writing or most unfairly ignored a whole clutch of writers who wrote for the very audience targeted and most valued by both Wells and himself. Think of R. H. Tawney, Harold Laski, G. D. H. Cole among academics, and H. N. Brailsford, Fenner Brockway, Kingsley Martin and Rebecca West among intellectual journalists. What was the audience? Wells and Orwell still called them 'the common man', those whom Virginia Woolf had called 'the common reader', an almost extinct species today. They were mainly those whose only university was the free public library.

My students, originally all part of post-war university expansion, found it hard to imagine that political books were once written in plain English not in social science, whether in the Marxiological or the American methodological dialect. Now we must raise the stakes a little, alas, and talk not of the common man (if he or she is politically literate it is now without the help of books) but of the general educated reader. Yet even for that narrower audience the case is the same. Consider that Penguin complete list. Indeed the age of reason seems over. The printed book now has a very much diminished role in preserving a citizen culture; or rather, I would say in Britain, in trying to create one. This country has never had a citizen culture, unlike France, The Netherlands or the United States.

Not for one moment do I wish to deny that there are a few fine good political writers who reach the general reader – such as Neal Ascherson, Ian Bell, Richard Harris, Christopher Hitchens, Will Hutton, Simon Jenkins, Richard Lipsey ('Bagehot' in *The Economist*), John Lloyd, Joyce Macmillan, Andrew Marr, Melanie Phillips, Polly Toynbee, Hugo Young. But any list, if impressive, will be short. I am using political writing to mean writing about political issues: reasoned advocacy. There have been some reasonably honest biographies of living politicians, say Ben Pimlott on Wilson and Rob Shepherd on Powell, if far more truly awful ones: uncritical popular hagiography of Wilson, Thatcher, Heseltine and even, Major and Blair. Such campaign biographies could be said to have marked the beginning of the Americanization of British campaigning. Leslie Smith's *Harold Wilson* of 1964 began these pious follies, a book hilariously funny for its earnest naivety. I wish the subjects of such books would do what a famous Tammony Hall Boss, Mayor Richard Croker, did when presented with such a book about himself as he was departing from New York to race his horses in Ireland: he read one page, threw it overboard into the Hudson and spat accurately.

The popularity now of almost any kind of biography is a

sad sign of the general debasement of the political and of civic culture: we all seem more interested in personality than in ideas. Robert McCrum has written shrewdly in *The Observer*, from his vantage point as literary editor, about the popularity of a new literature of celebrity narcissism, 'the high octane autobiographical memoir'. Private introspection turning into public exhibitionism as the sign of authentic personality seems to replace other-regarding concerns with public values. How often does one hear people sneer behind the backs of anyone exhibiting public spirit, 'there must be something wrong with them inwardly'. It is axiomatic that behind every activist there must be an unhappy home and/or sex life. Richard Sennett in his *The Fall of Public Man* put all this more kindly as 'narcissism is the Protestant ethic of modern times' (Sennett, 1986). Political leaders have for long tried to personify their parties, but suddenly we begin to suspect that they are only off-the-peg personalities, not even pretending to be persuasive, speculative popular thinkers. Nevertheless, there is a kind of well-written book about politics that often has little directly to do with analysis or advocacy of policy: I would call them political travel books. I note, not entirely happily, that the Orwell book prize for political writing each year for four years went to such a book: Anatol Lieven's *The Baltic Revolution*, Fionnuala O Connor's *In Search of the State*, Fergal Keane, *Season of Blood: A Rwandan Journey*, and Peter Godwin, *Mukiwa: A White Boy in Africa*. The fine writing as well as the moral integrity is commendable; but there were few books before us like the good old Penguin Specials. Penguin in the 1960s and into the early 1970s had three or four books a year on social problems that were political issues. Their general character was an informed and factual exposition of the problem, then a discussion of alternative policies and the principles governing them, followed by a reasoned and principled advocacy. Demand fell off. In another series for another publisher I once commissioned April Carter's *The Politics of Women's Rights* specifically to try to assess what had been achieved, the value of it all as well as the extent (Carter, 1988).

It was an admirable, clearly written book. It got many course adoptions in Women's Studies or general Politics courses, but I never met or heard of anyone who had read it outside a university course. This is not just a particular and personal grumble but a common tale

Some of the reasons for the decline of the political book are fairly obvious. The demand is, indeed, simply not there. Radio is now infinitely more venturesome and lively both in informative analysis and political advocacy than ever it was in the 1930s and 1940s. Television, after a slow start, developed likewise. The broadsheets today carry far more features and commentary than before the war, even if extensive reportage, sometimes even basic reportage, has suffered. We are also in a great age of the political column. Most intelligent people take most of their political ideas from the media, and perhaps something filters down from the excellence of the academy. But there are problems on the supply side too. Penguin tell me that they would publish more thoughtful political books for the general reader if they could find the authors. Most academics only write for other academics, and even if they could write for the general reader, do not want to; there is a professional hang-up about popularizing (very odd for politics, when there are currently excellent popularizers of science, and of history too). To be fair to publishers, the calculator does sometimes get put aside in favour of the civic hunch: a number of quite unlikely houses have felt that they must have, and chanced their arm on, a book on the Northern Ireland question – and usually lost it, or at least a bony finger or two. And perhaps I am not being fair to a few small socialist presses, like Spokesman in Nottingham, who do not write in Marxiological English, but still have in mind the old extra-mural class and trade union activist kind of audience. But I suspect their public is small. No more than political theatre does it radiate out to the wider reading public.

If the quality media drain the market for political books, one could say 'so what' and does it matter? It does matter because the complexity of social problems is hard to grasp and convey amid the diurnal galloping myopia of the broadsheets, let alone the papers that Middle England reads. Politicians on all sides use ever greater simplifications and sloganeering – 'soundbite politics' indeed. They know the public knows no more than they do, unless some problem encounters professional interests. Politicians and political editors, even, rarely feel that a book is a political event – other than a leading politician's memoirs, and these then rarely get reviewed properly even in the broadsheets, but are usually surrendered to another old politician ill-equipped, even if willing, to probe for the truth as a historian or a political scientist might (Crick, 1978 and 1993). Let me return to the paradox in all this. Never fewer political books, but never more political knowledge. The social sciences have found out a lot and do have much to say. Only economists, however, seem to be taken seriously outside academia. And yet we are in a great period of political thought. But in both cases it is academics talking to academics. There are no incentives to talk out to the public. Partly academics are themselves to blame: the way they write in jargon, and the way books are composed with evidence and argument all formidably interwoven, unlike the old Royal Commission reports and the better Select Committees or public inquiries where the argument and conclusions are set out simply for all who care to read, and the detailed evidence and submissions follow in appendices for all who care to check or think again.

If too many social scientists find plain English difficult (there is a tradition of plain writing among English political philosophers, for which at least we can thank the analytical school, even the logical positivists), there is also a political illiteracy among literary intellectuals. Books that should get reviewed in the broadsheets remain unknown outside academic journals like *Political Studies*, the *British Journal of Political Science*, *Political Theory*, etc. Of course space does not allow. But consider how some of the space is used. Even the truly seminal books get missed. Too many literary editors do not know a hawk from a handsaw, just as a few of my old colleagues would not know a Margaret Drabble from an A. S. Byatt. Other grass does look somewhat greener. Intellectuals have a higher standing in France and are expected to have views on public questions, sometimes with ludicrous or unfortunate results, true; but at least there is an intelligent commentary that is not merely an alternative to the academy, but often mediates the academy with a foot in both worlds. In Germany the far more regional structure of the Press than in England and Wales and the high quality of the regional papers leads to the use of more professors and intellectuals (not always the same, by any means) as feature writers or columnists. In the United States the sheer numbers of those who have had higher education allows for more non-disciplinary serious political publishing, not only about practical politics: 'public intellectuals' flourish, good and bad, writing about issues of principle, those endless and often quite good inquests into the state of the nation and the national psychology.

In Britain the Press makes no remedial attempts even occasionally to survey, summarize, translate what is important in the political knowledge and thought of the academy. *New Society* used to try. Specialists in the social science disciplines could then be understood by anyone intelligent, and by each other. And political and social philosophy were regularly reviewed, with a strong hint from the books editor to go light on disciplinary in-fighting and strong on fair précis. For a while *New Society* was analogous to *New Scientist*. But when the *New Statesman* took it over, all that vanished. Surveys of the social sciences would be possible as a regular weekly page in a broadsheet, but reading around would be a full-time job for someone with an unusual academic width and some journalistic talent. This is done for medicine but not for (scholarly) politics.

If some political philosophers think I stray far from political philosophy, then they either miss my point or are the fair targets of my double-edged polemic. The broad cultural and structural factors of society may not always determine what the academy studies, and should not. Freedom of scholarly inquiry and the diffusion of it is not merely a key test of civil freedom and good government, it is a necessary condition for it. But there is something wrong either with the academy or with journalists and politicians if this kind of knowledge and kind of critical skill in sharpening and clarifying the concepts used in political debate are not diffused, have no effect. As a scholar and a citizen I am pessimistically even-handed. There is something wrong with both. Neither seems to care to try. Both will suffer, as the public and polity suffer already from acute debasement of the language of political debate. Can the schools now gradually raise the standards and build firm bridges?

11 A meditation on democracy

This was the opening address to a conference at Oxford
in 1996 of the UNESCO International University, Tokyo,
and published in translation in Takashi Inoguchi (ed.),
The Changing Nature of Democracy (UNU Press, Tokyo,
1998).

Democracy is both a sacred and a promiscuous word. We all
love her but she is hard to pin down. Everyone claims her but
no one actually possesses her fully. A moment's thought will
remind us why this is so.

Historically there have been four broad usages. The first is
found in the Greeks, in Plato's attack on it and in Aristotle's
highly qualified defence: democracy is simply, in the Greek,
demos (the mob, the many) and *cracy*, meaning rule. Plato
attacked this as being the rule of the poor and the ignorant
over the educated and the knowledgeable, ideally philosophers. His fundamental distinction was between knowledge
and opinion: democracy is the rule, or rather the anarchy, of
mere opinion. Aristotle modified this view rather than reject-
ing it utterly: good government was a mixture of elements, the
few ruling with the consent of the many. The few should have
aristoi, the principle of excellence, the idealized concept of
aristocracy. But many more can qualify for citizenship by
virtue of some education and some property (both of which he
thought necessary conditions for citizenship), and so must be
consulted and can, indeed, even occasionally be promoted to

office. He did *not* call his 'best possible' state 'democracy' at all, rather *politea* or polity, or 'mixed-government', a political community of citizens deciding on common action by public debate. But democracy could be the next best thing in practice if it observed 'ruling and being ruled in turn'. But as a principle, when unchecked by aristocratic experience and knowledge, democracy was a fallacy: 'that because men are equal in some things, they are equal in all'.

The second usage is found in the Romans, in Machiavelli's great *Discourses*, in the seventeenth-century English and Dutch republicans and in the early American republic: that good government is mixed government, just as in Aristotle's theory, but that the democratic popular element could actually give greater power to a state. Good laws to protect all are not good enough unless subjects became active citizens making their own laws collectively. The argument was both moral and military. The moral argument is the more famous: both Roman paganism and later Protestantism had in common a view of man as an active individual, a maker and shaper of things, not just a law-abiding well-behaved acceptor or good subject of a traditional order. (It was this disjunction that so concerned the late Maruyama Masao in all his major essays on modernism and traditionalism.)

The third usage is found in the rhetoric and events of the French Revolution and in the writings of Jean-Jacques Rousseau – that everyone, regardless of education or property, has a right to make his or her will felt in matters of state; and indeed the general will or common good is better understood by any well-meaning, simple, unselfish and natural ordinary person from their own experience and conscience than by the overeducated living amid the artificiality of high society. Now this view can have a lot to do with the liberation of a class or a nation, whether from oppression or ignorance and superstition, but it is not necessarily connected with individual liberty. (In the European eighteenth and nineteenth centuries, remember, most people who cared for liberty did not call themselves democrats at all – constitutionalists or civic republicans, or, in the Anglo-American discourse, Whigs). The general will could have more to do with popularity than with representative institutions. Napoleon was a genuine heir of the French Revolution when he said that 'the politics of the future will be the art of stirring the masses'. His popularity was such, playing on both revolutionary and nationalist rhetoric, that he was able for the very first time to introduce mass conscription – that is to trust the common people with arms. The autocratic Hapsburgs and Romanovs had to be most careful to whom and where they applied selective conscription.

The fourth usage of democracy is found in the American constitution and in many of the new constitutions in Europe in the nineteenth century and in the new West German and Japanese constitutions following the Second World War; also in the writings of John Stuart Mill and Alexis de Tocqueville: that all can if they care, but must mutually respect the equal rights of fellow citizens within a regulatory legal order that defines, protects and limits those rights.

What most people today in the United States, Europe and Japan ordinarily mean by 'democracy' is ideally a fusion (but quite often a confusion) of the idea of power of the people and the idea of legally guaranteed individual rights. The two should, indeed, be combined, but they are distinct ideas, and can prove so in practice. There can be, and have been, intolerant democracies and reasonably tolerant autocracies. Personally, I do not find it helpful to call the system of government under which I live 'democratic'. To do so begs the question. It can close the door on discussion of how the actual system could be made more democratic, just as others once feared – and some still do so – that the democratic element becomes too powerful. Sociologically and socially England is still in many ways a profoundly undemocratic society (Scotland and Wales are somewhat more democratic), certainly when compared to the United States. But even in the United States there is overall now little citizenship or positive participation in politics in the republican style of the early American Republic. There are some interesting but very localized experiments in direct democracy, local referenda and 'citizenship panels', et cetera, and of course people vote (albeit in perpetually disappointing numbers) in formal elections, but between elections talk of and active participation in politics rates far, far lower as the most favoured national activity, apart from work, than shopping.

When considering the present nature and problems of democracy, I want to suggest that what we often mean to talk about is something even prior to either ideal or empirically observed definitions of democracy – politics itself. Here we all must have something to say. Politics is too important to be left to politicians. Politicians are too busy and preoccupied with – in the broad perspective of human history – short-term advantages and actions, with winning the next election, so others must speculate and try to do their long-term thinking about civilized humanity for them. Thought and action must go together, not merely if the political tradition is to be preserved but also, since the need is pressing, if it is to be extended. *By the political tradition I mean simply the activity of resolving disputes and determining policy politically, that is by public debate among free citizens.* Although this activity is one of the most important and celebrated inventions of human civilization, it is now so much taken for granted or even regarded – because of the actions of particular democratic politicians – as a debased activity; and party leaders in autocracies or in one-party states see it, when present among their followers, as a dangerous activity. In so many countries any opposition to the policies or leaders gets represented as opposition to the state itself. The beneficial application of politics is neither universal nor universally understood; or even if understood, it is not always desired or tolerated.

The political tradition may be the world's best hope, perhaps last hope as we see long-term problems begin to accumulate that could destroy (the phrase does have real meaning) civilization as we know it. If political solutions, or rather – as is ever the case, political compromises – are not found, power blocs will struggle harder and harder, more and more ruthlessly and competitively, in a world of increasing demands and of diminishing resources, to maintain the standard of living of at least a voting majority of their own loyal inhabitants. And it is necessary to remind ourselves that the misapplication of scientific and industrial technology now gives us these unique and handy opportunities for mutual destruction (quite apart from the slow but sure despoilation of the resources and natural environment that sustain us). The two World Wars of the twentieth century should have been a perfectly adequate demonstration of this, but could yet prove an inadequate premonition of the shape of things to come. During the Cold War, the fear of global destruction by atomic bombardment perhaps took the minds of most political leaders and thinkers off other slower global threats. And politically the post-war era has seen some good reasons for political optimism about the internal affairs of states. The collapse of Soviet power through sheer inefficiency, the somewhat similar decline, at least, of military regimes in Southern Europe and South America; and some relaxation of despotism in the largest country in the world, China, and some signs of civic stirrings even in the bloody anarchy of sub-equatorial Africa, are some such indicators. The new South African constitution is a great example of how political compromise is possible in what once seemed a hopeless situation of either continued oppression or destructive revolution. And generally the myth of the superior efficiency and the invincibility of power of totalitarian and autocratic states has been exploded.

However, the collective inability of democratic states to act together by political agreement to deal with real and vital common problems has been amply demonstrated also. Consider the inadequate response to the bloody shambles of the break-up of the Yugoslavian Federation, the lack of enforcement of United Nations resolutions on Israel, let alone failure so far to achieve effective international co-operation to prevent degradation of the environment of the whole planet. Take also the case of nuclear weapons: if the threat of deliberate two-bloc world war now seems happily (if

195

somewhat fortuitously) gone, yet the ability of the so-called great powers to prevent the spread of nuclear bombs to less stable regimes is now diminished almost to the point of impotence. Some of this impotence arises, of course, from the inability or unwillingness of political leaders in democracies (one in particular) to educate and change public opinion (precisely what Aristotle feared in 'democracy').

The invention, and then the tradition, of governing by means of political debate among citizens has its roots in the practices and thought of the Greek *polis* and the ancient Roman republic. So political rule could be said to be as 'Western' or 'European' in its origins, and yet as universal in its application, as natural science. But the origins of even such powerful and influential traditions of activity endow the descendants of its progenitors with no special wisdom, indeed sometimes it gives them a false sense of superiority and dangerous overconfidence. The general ideas of both political rule and of the natural sciences and attendant technologies are not bound to any one culture, have spread universally both as power-driven exports and as eagerly sought-after modernizing imports. The results, of course, vary greatly in different cultural settings and by the accidents of contingent events; but there is more in common now because of such a process between such societies than in the pre-political, pre-scientific and industrial world. The Eastern World may produce, almost certainly will, variants of the 'democratic', or as I prefer to say 'political' tradition, from which the West may learn – this has already happened in technology. But, it is fair to say, the West does not stand still entirely. That the concept of 'citizen' has been only fairly recently extended to women is no small matter – full civic equality is still far ahead, and the consequences of this are likely to be as great in the future as they are still unclear in the present. Now this elevated view of politics may surprise our fellow citizens who form their idea of 'the political' from what they read in their national newspapers about the behaviour, in all respects, of actual politicians. Indeed one must ask, are such politicians the friends or the foes of good government? Certainly they are (to use a favourite word of Hannah Arendt's) thoughtless about the consequences in terms of public example of how they practise politics and behave themselves, which is part of politics.

* * *

More than thirty years ago I wrote a book called *In Defence of Politics* which has remained in print until last year, and was translated into many languages including Japanese (thanks to Maruyama Masao). But it received few reviews by my then academic colleagues in Britain. But that did not dismay me for I had aimed the book at the intelligent general reader, and it has been called, if only by the publishers (but respectable and sensible people), 'a modern classic'. But what does dismay me is that during the last thirty years there has been a continuing decline in book publishing of serious political thinking aimed at and read by the public, despite all the troubles and unexpected opportunities of our times. Coherent political thinking can be all but abandoned by party leaders, certainly debased and too often reduced to soundbites uttered with a coached sincerity, but with no well-grounded justifications advanced for the fragments of general principles somewhat (or almost wholly) opportunistically advanced. Sincerity stands in for reasoning and when politics is discussed, even by intelligent ordinary people, it is more often discussed in terms of personalities than of principles and of appeals to immediate self-interest rather than to long-term mutual or public benefits. Only a few columnists and editorial writers in newspapers of some quality keep up the once prevalent tradition of intelligent and reasonably open-minded public debate and speculation.

During that same time the academic discipline of political thought, however, has thrived as never before, both as the history and contextualization of ideas and as the analysis of meaning and implications of concepts in current use – say freedom, equality, justice, sovereignty, nation, individualism, community and so on. But this advance has been almost

wholly internalized. Most academic writing on politics and
the problems of democracy can be seen, sometimes rather
generously, as contributions to the advancement of knowledge, as well as to the individual's reputation and promotion
prospects; but few seem interested in diffusing this knowledge
to the public (or, if so, are able to do so). Faults on both sides
can be found: it is all too easy to make a career by writing
about politics ('researching' is now the term more frequently
used) and yet for the product to remain wholly within the
ivory tower, unknown either to the press or to the reading
public. The irony of doing this for the study of politics escapes
most of the denizens of the castle. We are often rather like
those student leaders of the 1960s who proclaimed their
solidarity with the working class and 'the people' in a Marxist
terminology understandable only to those among 'the people'
who had a degree in social science at a new university. But, on
the other hand, the media take very few steps to discover and
use the academic product. In Britain only the talents of experts
on electoral statistics are regularly courted. The idea is strange
to leader writers that there is a tradition of political thinking
and knowledge as relevant to the problems of the modern
world as economic theory, and one historically more important. Political considerations are far more often held to
interfere with economic reasoning than the contrary.

The thesis of my *In Defence of Politics* was all too easy even
if challengingly simple. It spoke of making some 'platitudes
pregnant': that politics is the conciliation of naturally different
interests, whether these interests are seen as material or moral,
usually both. I wrote in the Aristotelian tradition. There is a
famous passage in Aristotle's *Politics* where he says that the
great mistake of his master Plato was in writing about ideal
states as if to find a single unifying principle of righteousness.
Rather,

> there is a point at which a *polis*, by advancing in unity, will cease
> to be a *polis*; but will none the less come near to losing its essence,
> and will thus be a worse *polis*. It is as if you were to turn harmony

into mere unison, or to reduce a theme to a single beat. The truth
is that the *polis* is an aggregate of many members.

Not all societies are organized and governed according to
political principles. Most governments in history suppress
public debate about policy, far preferring to encourage 'good
subjects' rather than good or active citizens. But this has
become more and more difficult in the modern world. Yet it
is not just so-called political ideologies that threaten free
politics; nationalism and religion can do so also. There is
nationalism and nationalism, religion and religion; sometimes reasonably tolerant, at other times intensely intolerant.
Although politics is not necessarily threatened by strong
religious belief, sometimes not even when there is a dominant religion, yet some beliefs and practices stifle or threaten
free politics and the open expression of contrary views. But
some secularists also can see politics as inherently disruptive
of social order. 'The country could be run better without all
this politics.' And many must sympathize with Dr Joseph
Goebbels's axiom: 'Politicians perpetuate problems, we seek
to solve them.'

So political rule, I remind, existed before democratic
government and is, in a very real sense, logically prior to
democracy, unless by that term we mean, rather fatuously,
'everything we would like' rather than a component of good
government, a concept of majority opinion and power that is
not always compatible with liberty and individual rights.
Some dictatorships, for instance, have been and still can be
genuinely popular, resting on majority support and the stronger for it. Both historically and logically, politics is prior to
democracy. We may want to fill the cart full of good things
that everyone wants and feels they need, but the horse must go
out in front. Without order there can be no democracy, and
without politics even democracy is unlikely to be just. Political
rule is the most generally justifiable type of order.

Therefore, still leaning on old Aristotle against the over-
sophistication of modern social science (whether in the

199

Marxist or the modern American mode), politics rests on two preconditions, a sociological and a moral. The sociological is that civilized societies are all complex and inherently pluralistic, even if and when (hopefully) the injustices of class, ethnic and gender discriminations will vanish or diminish. The moral aspect was that it is normally better to conciliate differing interests than to coerce and oppress them perpetually, or seek to remove them without consent or negotiated compensation. While much political behaviour is prudential, there is always some moral context: some compromises we think it wrong to make, and some possible ways of coercion or even of defence which we think are too cruel, disproportionate or simply too uncertain. A nuclear first strike, for example, even against a non-nuclear power, could not reasonably be called political behaviour – even against Baghdad. Hannah Arendt was wiser than Clausewitz and his disciple Dr Kissinger when she said that violence is the breakdown of politics, not (in his famous aphorism) its 'continuance by other means'.

So it was too easy for me to argue that it is always better to be governed politically, if there is any choice in the matter. The thesis did not seem so banal or simple-minded at the time because there was sustained contrast, in some passages explicit but implicit all through, between political rule and totalitarian rule. The simple could then appear both profound and important. But with the breakdown of Soviet power and the old pull towards a binary system, the whole world has become more complicated and previously existing contradictions in the so-called free world have both come to the surface and grown more acute. (I am not too happy with 'free world', by the way, for that concept – like 'our democratic way' – begs far too many questions, makes too many assumptions, is a highly complex concept whose components need unpacking and testing carefully for quality, and is too often self-righteous and propagandistic in use; so to say rather those parts of the world that are ruled politically. But the concept of politics certainly implies freedom and its widespread practice depends upon it.)

Just as totalitarian rule and ideology could break down internally, so can political rule; and political prudence can prove inadequate. I gave such situations little serious attention in my *In Defence* ... Since then I have studied both in books, documents and newspapers and by talking to people on the ground, the conflicts in Northern Ireland, South Africa and Israel/Palestine, turning what were originally accidental encounters into deliberate commitments. Each is so different in detail but they have shared a problem in common. So I use them symbolically as *examples* of the general problem of the adequacy of 'mere politics' when people who enjoy at least some kind of a political tradition, yet refuse any talk of compromise, because they feel that their *very identity* is at stake if they give any ground. They can have a conviction that they are on the very edge of 'a step too far' if their leaders even talk to their enemies and that they could then 'fall from a great height'.

The justification of politics in terms of the negation of totalitarianism was all too easy. The mundane could be made melodramatic in terms of contrast. The 'defeat' of the USSR and the 'victory' of the West also appeared to imply the rejection and then the demise of ideology. I took ideology to be not any set of specific ideas about particular things (say beliefs and doctrines) but secular claims to comprehensive explanation and policy. Old autocracies, however bigoted, bloody and cruel, had limited aspirations – usually just for the ruling class to stay in power and so sleeping dogs could lie if they paid their taxes and doffed their hats. But some modern autocracies earned the new name because they saw the need to mobilize the masses, to make sleeping dogs bark and even sing in unison, to attempt to achieve the revolutionary objectives of an ideology. But ideology did *not* vanish with the demise of Communist power and its universalistic pretensions. Political prudence and pragmatism did not take over. Rather there emerged the rapid, almost wildfire spread of the belief that more-or-less unrestrained market forces will resolve all major problems on a global scale; or at any rate that they cannot be resisted. If Adam Smith was read, it was without his moral philosophy that was the explicit context for the beneficent working of markets.

Hannah Arendt in her great book *The Human Condition* remarked that there have only ever been two kinds of comprehensive ideologies claiming to hold the key to history: the belief that all is determined by *race* and the belief that all is determined by *economics*. Both racism and economicism are, we should remember, distinctively modern beliefs: before the late eighteenth century the world could get by without such enormous secular claims, and not even religions claimed to *explain* everything. Arendt pointed out that economic ideology took two rival forms, and yet their belief that there must be a *general system* had a common origin and linked them more than their disciples believe: *Marxism* (all is class owner-ship) and *laissez-faire* (all is market forces). The missionaries and advocates of market ideology in the former Soviet bloc now denounce political interventions in the economy almost as fiercely as did the old totalitarians, although fortunately they are still subject to some political restraints and a few residual cultural inhibitions. In the party politics of the moment in my own country my friends rightly rail against excesses of privatization, the diminishment of public welfare from the state and the attacks of a government on the very concept of a *res publica* or a public interest. Governments can seek to distance themselves from any responsibility for guiding Adam Smith's hidden hand by which the free market becomes the public interest (give or take some emmolient oils of private charity and rituals of religious benevolence – thinking of the real Adam Smith). But in a broader perspective, the degree of political restraint upon the children of Hayek – the Reagans and the Thatchers – is also remarkable. They have done to us, for good or ill, much less than they know they ought to have done; and that is because of 'irrational political factors', thank God!

Prices cannot be sensibly determined except by market mechanisms; the final breakdown of Soviet planning proved that – however well it may have served for a time of emergency. And capitalism is an international system whose imperatives can be ignored only at a fearful price – say North Korea and Cuba, or by the luck, while it lasts, of oil in the sand. But it does not then follow that price must determine every human relationship, least of all the civic. The effects of the market can be either limited or mitigated by civic action; some should be. *Man is citizen as well as consumer.* There is taxation, for instance; there is or was public and family morality, strong cultural restraints on the exercise of both economic and political power. New lines of demarcation and mutual influence between the polity and the economy need examining closely and coolly. If people see themselves purely as consumers they will lose all real control of government. Governments will then rule by bread and circuses, even if not by force; and torrents of trivial alternatives will make arbitrary and often meaningless choice pass for effective freedom. For all the absolutist rhetoric, in reality at least a degree of welcome confusion reigns. Only the two extreme positions of All-State or All-Market are untenable; there is a lot of space between. Political and economic factors and principles interact with each, limit each other; but neither can live for long without the other.

Of course it was always foolish in the light of history to think that the end of the Cold War (a quite sudden event that neither prophets nor social scientists expected – a salutary warning to all prophets disguised as social scientists) would by itself lead to peace, prosperity, freedom. And what new democracy has emerged looks much more like Schumpeter's view of democracy as a competitive electoral struggle between party elites (Schumpeter, 1942) than the old republican ideal that inhabitants and subjects should all become active, participative and critical citizens.

Consider, by way of contrast to even the best democratic practices of today, a passage that used to be worrying knowledge to autocrats and elites in Europe, and a source of inspiration to their opponents, especially the American

Republic's founding fathers. Once upon a time the Periclean oration of the fifth century BC in Athens as recounted by Thucydides would have been read by almost everyone who read books at all:

> Our constitution is called a democracy because power is in the hands not of a minority but of the whole people. When it is a question of settling private disputes, every one is equal before the law; when it is a question of putting one person before another in positions of public responsibility, what counts is not membership of a particular class, but the actual ability which the man possesses. No one, so long as he has it in him to be of service to the state, is kept in political obscurity because of poverty. And, just as our political life is free and open, so is our day-to-day life in our relations with each other. We do not get into a state with our next-door neighbour if he enjoys himself in his own way, nor do we give him the kind of black looks which, though they do no real harm, still do hurt people's feelings. We are free and tolerant in our private lives; but in public affairs we keep to the law. This is because it commands our deep respect ...
>
> Here each individual is interested not only in his own affairs but in the affairs of the state as well: even those who are mostly occupied with their own business are extremely well-informed on general politics – this is a peculiarity of ours: we do not say that a man who takes no interest in politics is a man who minds his own business; we say that he has no business here at all. We Athenians, in our own persons, take our decisions on policy or submit them to proper discussions: for we do not think that there is an incompatibility between words and deeds; the worst thing is to rush into action before the consequences have been properly debated ...   (Thucydides, 1974)

Historians now assert, of course, that Pericles must be understood as a demagogue, a kind of democratic dictator. But the point for us is what the demagogue said, what he knew people wanted to hear, the lasting ideal he invoked, not what he did or why he said it. As Swift said, 'hypocrisy is the tribute that vice pays to virtue'.

References

Advisory Group on Citizenship (1998) *Education for Citizenship and the Teaching of Democracy in Schools* (London: QCA).

Alibhai-Brown, Yasmin (1999) *True Colours: Public Attitudes to Multi-Culturalism and the Role of Government* (London: Institute of Public Policy Research).

Annette, John (1999) 'Citizenship and higher education', in Denis Lawton and Roy Gardner (eds) *Values in Education* (London: Kogan Page).

Arendt, Hannah (1958) 'The public and the private realm', in her *The Human Condition* (London: Cambridge University Press).

Arendt, Hannah (1970) 'Karl Jaspers, citizen of the world', in her *Men in Dark Times* (London: Jonathan Cape).

Aristotle (1948) *The Politics* (ed. Ernest Barker) (Oxford: Oxford University Press).

Berlin, Sir Isaiah (1958) *Two Concepts of Liberty* (Oxford: Clarendon Press) and in his anthology (1997) *The Proper Study of Mankind* (Oxford: Oxford University Press).

Brennan, Tom (1981) *Political Education and Democracy* (Cambridge: Cambridge University Press).

Buckingham-Hatfield, Susan with Annette, John and Slater-Simmons, Elaine (1999) *Student Community Partnerships in Higher Education* (London: CSV).

Carter, April (1988) *The Politics of Women's Rights* (London: Longman).

Collini, Stefan (1991) *Public Moralists: Political Thought and Intellectual Life in Britain 1850–1930* (Oxford: Clarendon Press).

Commission on Citizenship (1990) *Encouraging Citizenship* (London: HMSO).

Crick, B. (1962 and 4th edn 1992) *In Defence of Politics* (London: Penguin).

References

Crick, B. (1968) 'Freedom as politics', in Peter Laslett and W. G. Runciman (eds) *Philosophy, Politics and Society* (Oxford: Blackwell).

Crick, B. (1971) 'Freedom as politics', in his *Political Theory and Practice* (London: Allen Lane).

Crick, B. (1974) 'Basic political concepts and curriculum development'. *Teaching Politics*, January, 13–24.

Crick, B. (1978) 'Commentary: political reviews'. *Political Quarterly*, July–September, 255–8.

Crick, B. (1993) 'Commentary: political reviewing'. *Political Quarterly*, October–December, 369–90.

Crick, B. (1995) 'The sense of identity of the indigenous British'. *New Community* 21(2), 167–82.

Crick, B. and Heater, Derek (1977) *Essays on Political Education* (Ringmer: Falmer Press).

Crick, B. and Porter, Alex (eds) (1978) *Political Education and Political Literacy* (London: Longman).

DfEE (1997) *Excellence in Education* (London: HMSO).

Freeden, M. (1978) *The New Liberalism* (Oxford: Oxford University Press).

Garnett, Mark (1993) 'An unheard voice in the squabbles of mankind'. *Political Quarterly*, July–September, 336–43.

Gellner, Ernest (1973) *Cause and Meaning in the Social Sciences* (London: Routledge), p. 49.

Gould, B. (1985) *Socialism and Freedom* (London: Macmillan).

Hahn, Caroline (1998) *Becoming Political: Comparative Perspectives on Citizenship Education* (Albany, NY: SUNY Press).

Hanniford, I. (1996) *Race: The History of an Idea in the West* (Baltimore: Johns Hopkins University Press).

Hargreaves, D. (1997) *The Mosaic of Learning* (London: Demos).

Heater, Derek (ed.) (1969) *The Teaching of Politics* (London: Methuen).

Heater, Derek (1984) *Peace Through Education: The Contribution of the Council for Education in World Citizenship* (London: Falmer Press).

Heater, Derek (1990) *Citizenship: The Civic Ideal in World History, Politics and Education* (London: Longman).

Heater, Derek (1996) *World Citizenship and Government: Cosmopolitan Ideas in the History of Western Political Thought* (London: Macmillan).

Hoggart, Richard (1999) *First and Last Things* (London: Aurum Press).

Holden, Cathie and Clough, Nick (1998) *Children as Citizens: Education for Participation* (London: Jessica Kingsley).

Hollins, T. H. B. (ed.) (1964) *Aims of Education: The Philosophical Approach* (Manchester: Manchester University Press).

Howarth, Alan (1992) 'Political education: a government view', in Bill Jones and Lynton Robins (eds) (1992) *Two Decades in British Politics: Essays to Mark Twenty-one Years of the Politics Association, 1969–90* (Manchester: Manchester University Press).

Ichilov, Orit (1998) *Citizenship and Citizenship Education in a Changing World* (London: Woburn Press).

Institute for Citizenship Studies (1998) 'Public attitudes towards citizenship' (a MORI survey commissioned by the Institute and published on their website: www.citizen.org.uk).

Jones, Bill and Robins, Lynton (eds) (1992) *Two Decades in British Politics: Essays to Mark Twenty-one Years of the Politics Association, 1969–90* (Manchester: Manchester University Press).

Kerr, David (1996) *Citizenship Education in Primary Schools* (London: Institute for Citizenship Studies).

Kerr, David (1999a) *Re-Examining Citizenship Education: The Case of England – National Case Study for IEA Citizenship Education Study Phase 1* (Slough: NFER).

Kerr, David (1999b) 'Re-examining citizenship education in England', in Judith Torney-Purta, John Schwille and Jo-Ann Amadeo, *Civic Education Across Countries: Twenty-four National Case Studies from the IEA Civic Education Project* (Amsterdam: IEA).

Kerr, David (1999c) 'Changing the political culture: the Advisory Group on Education for Citizenship and the teaching of democracy in schools'. *Oxford Review of Education*, 25(1, 2), March and June (special issue on Political Education), 275–84.

Laski, Harold (1925) *A Grammar of Politics* (London: Allen and Unwin).

Lippmann, Walter (1914) *A Preface to Politics* (New York: McGraw-Hill).

Lippmann, Walter (1954) *The Public Philosophy* (Boston: Little, Brown).

Lister, Ian (1987) 'Political education in England'. *Teaching Politics*, 16(1), 19–27.

References

Marshal, T. H. (1950) *Citizenship and Social Class and Other Essays* (Cambridge: Cambridge University Press).

Modood, Tariq (1992) *The Difficulties of Being English* (Trentham: Trentham Books).

Modood, Tariq, Beison, Sharon and Verdee, Satnam (1994) *Changing Ethnic Identities* (London: Policy Studies Institute).

Nairn, Tom (1988) *The Enchanted Glass: Britain and its Monarchy* (London: Century Hutchinson).

National Curriculum Council (1990) *Education for Citizenship: Guidance Paper No. 5* (York: NCC (now QCA)).

Niebuhr, Reinhold (1954) *Christian Realism and Politics* (London: Faber).

Oakshott, Michael (1962) 'Political education', in his *Rationalism and Other Essays* (London: Methuen).

Oldfield, Adrian (1990) *Citizenship and Community: Civil Republicanism and the Modern World* (London: Routledge).

Oliver, Dawn and Heater, Derek (1994) *The Foundations of Citizenship* (London: Harvester/Wheatsheaf).

Orwell, George (1941) *The Lion and the Unicorn: Socialism and the English Genius* (London: Secker & Warburg).

Orwell, George (1949) *Nineteen Eighty-Four* (London: Secker & Warburg).

Orwell, George (1994) 'Wells, Hitler and the world state', in *The Penguin Essays of George Orwell* (Harmondsworth: Penguin), p. 190. (An essay first published in 1938.)

Ostler, Audrey with Starkey, Hugh (1996) *Teacher Education and Human Rights* (London: David Fulton).

Ostler, Audrey (1996) *Learning to Participate: Human Rights, Citizenship and Development in the Local Community* (Birmingham: Development Education Centre).

Oxford Review of Education (1999) 'Political education' (special issue), 25(1, 2), March and June.

Patterson, Lindsay (1994) *The Autonomy of Modern Scotland* (Edinburgh: Edinburgh University Press).

Philp, M. (1999) 'Citizenship and integrity', in A. Montefiori and D. Vines (eds) *Integrity in Public and Private Domains* (London: Routledge), pp. 19–21.

Pierce, Nick and Hallgarten, Joe (eds) (2000) *Tomorrow's Citizens: Critical Debates in Citizenship and Education* (London: Institute for Public Policy Research).

Pocock, John (1975) *The Machiavellian Moment: Florentine Political Thought and the Atlantic Republican Tradition* (Princeton, NJ, and London: Princeton University Press).

Popper, Sir Karl (1963) *Refutations and Conjectures* (London: Routledge).

Rawls, John (1972) *A Theory of Justice* (Oxford: Clarendon Press).

Ricci, David M. (1984) *The Tragedy of Political Science* (London: Yale).

Rose, E. J. B. *et al.* (1969) *Colour and Citizenship: A Report on Race Relations* (Oxford: Oxford University Press).

Runciman, W. G. (1966) *Relative Deprivation and Social Justice* (London: Routledge).

Sennett, Richard (1986) *The Fall of Public Man* (London: Faber and Faber).

Skinner, Quentin (1998) *Liberty Before Liberalism* (Cambridge: Cambridge University Press).

Slater, John (1992) 'New curricula, new directions', in Bill Jones and Lynton Robins (eds) *Two Decades of British Politics* (Manchester: Manchester University Press), pp. 305–17.

Snook, I. A. (ed.) (1972a) *Concepts of Indoctrination: Philosophical Essays* (London: Routledge).

Snook, I. A. (1972b) *Indoctrination and Education* (London: Routledge).

Spencer, Sarah and Bynoe, Ian (1998) *A Human Rights Commission: The Options for Britain and Northern Ireland* (London: Institute for Public Policy Research).

Thucydides (1974) *The Peloponnesian War* (London: Penguin), p. 177.

Torney-Purta, Judith, Schwille, John and Amadeo, Jo-Ann (1999) *Civic Education Across Countries: Twenty-four National Case Studies from the IEA Civic Education Project* (Amsterdam: IEA).

Toulmin, S. (1972) *Human Understanding*, Vol. 1 (Oxford: Clarendon Press).

Wallace, William (1997) *Why Vote Liberal Democrat?* (London: Penguin).

Whitebrook, Maureen (1991) *Reading Political Stories: Representations of Politics in Novels and Pictures* (Lankam, Maryland: Rowman and Littlefield).

Whitebrook, Maureen (1995) *Real Toads in Imaginary Gardens:*

Narrative Accounts of Liberalism (London: Rowman and Littlefield).

Willetts, David (1997) *Why Vote Conservative?* (London: Penguin).

Winch, P. (1958) *The Idea of a Social Science* (London: Routledge), p. 58.

Wolin, Sheldon S. (1960) *Politics and Vision* (London: Allen and Unwin).

Wright, Tony (1997) *Why Vote Labour?* (London: Penguin).

Young, Michael (1958) *The Rise of Meritocracy* (Harmondsworth: Penguin).